BEYOND
—— THE ——
WIND
CHIMES

BEYOND
— THE —
WIND
CHIMES

A Collection of Short Stories and Reflections

PHYLLIS ADAIR WARD

iUniverse®

BEYOND THE WIND CHIMES
A COLLECTION OF SHORT STORIES AND REFLECTIONS

The Authorized (King James) Version of the Bible ('the KJV'), the rights in which are vested in the Crown in the United Kingdom, is reproduced here by permission of the Crown's patentee, Cambridge University Press. The Cambridge KJV text including paragraphing, is reproduced here by permission of Cambridge University Press.

iUniverse books may be ordered through booksellers or by contacting:

iUniverse
1663 Liberty Drive
Bloomington, IN 47403
www.iuniverse.com
1-800-Authors (1-800-288-4677)

ISBN: 978-1-5320-1128-3 (sc)
ISBN: 978-1-5320-1129-0 (e)

Library of Congress Control Number: 2016918786

Print information available on the last page.

iUniverse rev. date: 11/23/2016

To My Great-Great-Grandchildren

My dear children,

If you are reading this, the world – at least where you are – has survived. Perhaps there is no one else who knows or cares of my existence. If there was a way of knowing and I think there is…I would be extremely pleased.

You came from a line of relatives who had a curiosity about everything.

What can I tell you that you can't find out with the click of whatever has replaced what is now called the mouse on my computer? You are probably looking through archives of some kind. Perhaps you found the old mother board from my ancient computer. I can't imagine what your search engine would be like.

What advice can I give you? I doubt that you would take it. I rarely did. I have no advice. Just this. You are loved with the same love that my great-great-grandmother had for me. How do you know? I have no doubt that you would ask that question. SHE THRIVED AND SURVIVED! As a result, you are here or there or whichever the case may be.

Stay strong. Your world needs strength, needs you and above all, it needs love! Never, ever forget the price your ancestors paid for you.

I love you with an everlasting love,

Grandmother,

Phyllis

The voice of parents is
the voice of God's,
for to their children
they are heaven's lieutenants.
William Shakespeare-

Contents

IN THE GARDEN

MOM

I WAS JUST THINKING

EVERY GOODBYE AIN'T GONE

A VERSION OF ESSAYS PRESENTED
TO A LADIES GROUP ESSAYS

Acknowledgements

This book, *Beyond The Wind Chimes*, was written 15 years after *Wind Chimes and Promises*. *Wind Chimes and Promises* was written in my mother's voice. This book is written in my voice. It includes poems, short stories, fiction, non-fiction, rants and a few goodbyes. Many thanks to everyone who has been a part of my life and as such, contributed to this work. There are so many.

Wind Chimes and Promises took me to places that I never thought I would go. I met **Laura Gaus**, teacher and author, who became my mentor and friend.

Ed Harris, minister, teacher, poet, activist who also became a friend. His wife, **Sandra Harris**, introduced me to storytelling and oral history. There were countless book reviews given for book clubs, libraries, churches, country clubs and a synagogue.

Rita Kohn, teacher, author, and playwright, turned a portion of *Wind Chimes and Promises* into a play. The play was at the Indiana State Museum and was sponsored at WFYI Studio and shown several times on WFYI TV, a public TV station, and on WFYI Radio. One of the stories from the book was included in a book called *Tapestry*. The little book written for my mother has been read as far as Afghanistan and Accra, Ghana Africa.

Linda Caldwell Lee, for her writing group. Linda has the ability to help you see a story in everything. In her class, I learned that there is a story in everything you see and touch.

Margaret Kallman, for her friendship, encouragement and typing skills.

James Patterson, an old friend who has always been supportive and who has taken the time to edit the book, just as he did on my first book.

It has been an enormous pleasure to meet people who have read *Wind Chimes and Promises* and know where Homer, Georgia, Banks County is. Listening to them speak and hearing their success is a taste of Mother's birthplace, and the taste is sweet in my mouth.

Beyond The Wind Chimes will probably never be read by as large an audience as my previous book. *Wind Chimes and Promises* was truly a miracle. I have no other explanation about how it all happened.

I will share this book with a few. I hope that you are one of them.

"O God, thou hast taught me from my youth: and
hitherto have I declared thy wondrous works." –
Psalm 71:17 – King James Version (KJV)

Beyond the Wind Chimes

This book is written in the hope that the reader will see the importance of recording "his/her" story. Everyone has one. Your family and friends deserve to read your story. You owe it to yourself to write it. No one can tell your story like you can.

"Now go, write it before them in a table, and note it in a book,
that it may be for the time to come for ever and ever:" –
Isaiah 30:8 – King James Version (KJV)

Dedicated to my husband Tom who is my love, my friend, my support, my rock, and a great joy to my life! As I have often said, "He was well worth the wait." **And to all of my children.**

Preface

Family. You cannot separate the powerful reverence for and appreciation of family when you talk of Phyllis Adair Ward. So it is not surprising that her first memoir, *Wind Chimes and Promises*, would chronicle her family's humble start in Homer, Georgia, through their confrontations in a race-discriminating South, and the triumphant escape and ultimate deliverance of the tyranny that confined them.

Phyllis' story is not limited to her family memoir. A lifelong writer and consummate observer of the world around her, *Beyond The Wind Chimes* continues her observations, her wonderful humor, and keen eye for the things that delight, entertain and prompt one to think. It is food for the soul.

Through this collection of short stories and poems, Phyllis gives us a deep awareness of her view of the world and connects with her readers by reaching them through common struggles, hurts and triumphs. Ever apparent is Phyllis' gentle and loving spirit as she reflects on the things that are most important to her – caring for others, being a lifelong learner and her deep faith.

Our ten-year friendship has been a gentle adoption into each other's families. When you are lucky enough to know Phyllis, – really **know** her – you are forever changed. Over the years, I have cherished my time with her, most often spent over a leisurely four-hour lunch where she has shared her latest writings. She has mentored, supported and motivated me through some of the biggest challenges of my life, and I am grateful for her wit, charm and the gentle ways she lends her life experiences so willingly.

Mary Beth Googasian

In Memory of My Parents

Jesse Morgan Adair, Sr.
Prudence Knox Adair

My Brother,
Jesse Morgan Adair, Jr.

You will always be in the very
best part of my memories

Love Includes . . .
Love Excludes

"For now we see through a glass, darkly; but then face to face: now
I know in part; but then shall I know even as also I am known.
"And now abideth faith, hope, charity, these three;
but the greatest of these is charity."
1 Corinthians 13:12-13
King James Version (KJV)

Introduction

I write because I want to see my thoughts on paper. The words seem to just hang around in my head with no place to put them. If I write the words, I can clear them from my mind. So many thoughts seem to bump into each other, fighting to be written or said aloud.

Once the words and thoughts are written, it makes room for more thoughts. I've often wondered why the words written are never as profound as they seemed to be in my head. One day, I hope someone, maybe my daughter, might find my words and be able to see my heart, and understand who I am.

Writing helps to be alert, to look for more words, more books, and more dictionaries. I simply love words, written or spoken. I love eloquent words.

I love the word "yet" because I see so many possibilities in that one word. I have been in so many situations where I prayed for the right words to say. *"Let the words of my mouth and the meditations of my heart be acceptable in thy sight, Oh Lord, my strength and my redeemer."* – Psalm 19:14 – King James Version (KJV).

I want to write acceptable or unacceptable words. I want to empty out my heart and soul on paper. That's my gift to the world; the only one I really have.

Many writers tell me that they write at least two hours a day. I wish I had that discipline. Writing certainly requires passion, and the ability to express oneself in a new and different way.

Find a writer who you admire and see if your writing styles are similar; I've heard. There are so many writers that I admire, I have read so many books. Books by James Baldwin and Richard Wright come to mind. I think that they wrote "their truth." Both did an outstanding job,

I think. There are some truths that I can't write about because it would be a betrayal to others. They must tell their own truths. For now, I must keep some truths locked away. I tried to do what was hardest for me and that was to write a few poems!

It takes courage to write your own truth. Often truth becomes novelized, and some biographies are exaggerated. Isn't that true of most books? I have written about things that have spoken to me. Some things have spoken louder than others.

The thoughts and stories in this book have been written at different times in my life. I hope that this book has given you a glimpse into my "truth." This will probably be the last book that I write. I am in my eighties now and can hardly wait to see the next step of my journey. Thank you for taking part of the journey with me. I feel so honored that you, my "friend" have read this book. I hope that some portion of the book made you smile and think of your own memories and always, TRUTH.

Phyllis

POEMS

River of Life

A child stood at the bank of a river contemplating. What will life hold?
There was no one there to answer.
"What is the purpose of life?" the child asked.
Deep within the recesses of the child's heart
lie self-buried truth and the purpose.
Like this child, many stand at a metaphoric river of life
and contemplation, wondering and searching.
What is the answer and what is the purpose?
Most of us really know, but, we don't want to walk in our purpose.
Is there a fear that binds us?
When we don't walk in our purpose, there is always a feeling
of disconnection, confusion, and inner restlessness.
If you really want to know your purpose, take the hand
of someone God-filled and wiser than yourself.
If not…you will always stand at the river of contemplation.
The past is just that…past! And the past died yesterday.
Today is a new day. Not to live and walk in
your purpose would be a waste.
YOU can change your life and the lives of
so many others. The world waits.
Don't stand at the river too long.

Gratitude

I am grateful I woke up this morning
and I was able to get up.
I have my own teeth and
I do not have to retrieve them from a cup.
Perhaps, that is something you can become accustomed to,
but I am glad I don't have to do it.

I am grateful and blessed to have a husband
who doesn't question some of the crazy things I do and
doesn't have a need to know where I am every minute.

I am grateful for my family and the legacy they have left for me.
I am grateful for true friends,
which are few.

I am certainly grateful for
the changing of the seasons,
though I hate to see Autumn go.

One Bitter Cold Day

It's bitter cold. I'm staying inside today
And watching cars pass my window.
Please stay. I need your warmth.
Let's wrap up in a blanket and listen to some music.

"Do you remember when we went to see
Miles Davis?"
It was a bitter cold evening.
He stood alone in the glowing spotlight of
A crowded smoke-filled room.

Dark, slender, broad-shouldered,
"Remember how he played with his back turned?"
We savored every sweet note that floated from
his trumpet.
Miles seemed oblivious to cheers and applause.
No one minded being ignored.
We understood he was in a place we couldn't enter.
Perhaps he was cold, wanted to stay "inside"
watching cars go by and bask in the warmth
of his own music.

Searching

Suddenly dark as midnight,
feeling the shock of it.
No smell or taste to it.
Piercingly quiet, can't move,
and shouldn't move.
Walk carefully, don't fall.
Dark, desperately dark. Can't think.
Just wait…CAN'T wait.
If you were here you would lead me
through the darkness
until I found the light.
A flash of light permeates
the darkness, thank you.
Now, I can find my way.
If only all of life could be that easy.

Blues

Her head moves slowly up and down
as she listens to the mellow sound of
the Blues.

She remembers hard lonely times.

Blues
born out of hardship. Yet so smooth
you can almost taste it.

Blues, swaying, toe tapping music!

Blues
So sad it seeps into every pore, stabs with
every breath, creeps into the marrow
of your bones.

Blues
Sung by singers with strange names
like Muddy Waters and Howling Wolf.

A party isn't a party until someone says
"Play Down Home Blues." "Yeah."

Muddy Water starts crooning on the Juke Box.
"Down home blues. Down home blues.
Sometimes you get those down home blues
all night long."

Now the party really gets started.

The rickety old juke joint seems to rock.
Lights are turned down low.

Bodies cling together in oppressive heat.
Problems are temporarily forgotten.

Blues
Not everyone can understand it.

Perhaps you think you have
never had the "Blues."

Everybody has had the "Blues."
Maybe you just didn't know
what to call it.

She knew what to call it.
That's why she swayed to the
mellow sound.

People Need Dreams

Dreams that will change you,
that will fulfill a longing.

Dreams that will bring completion to a task undone.
Dreams about risks you were too afraid to
take when you were younger.

Dreams that seemed too grandiose to ever come to fruition.

Dreams that gave you joy and happiness.

Dreams about a poem or book you yearn to write.
Dreams unshared and unspoken 'til now.

Dreams about a day with blue skies, white clouds, birds
singing, butterflies flying, chipmunks playing.

A quiet day to rest, reflect, and give thanks that you can spend
a day just dreaming. No phone calls, no knocks at the door, no
grocery shopping, cleaning, or doing laundry, no budget list
needed. Just a day to dream and speak to yourself out loud.

People need dreams. Without them, there is
really no need to wake up, or get up.

Without a dream, you are like ships without a compass, sailing aimlessly without direction.

Dare to dream a dream that may seem preposterous to others, but it's your dream.

So dream well. People need dreams.

The Hands That Gave So Much

Your steel gray mane of hair cut short.
Tired eyes
Bone weary
Yet stately, valiant, courageous, hopeful
How many surgeries have there been?
I can't remember.
You smiled when I touched your hands.
The hands that gave so much
You gave joy, encouragement and laughter.
At 1 p.m. the nurse pulls your bed towards another surgery.
You say this will be the last.
I will see you later.
I throw you a kiss, you blow one back.
Eight hours later – I touch your hands, one across
your chest, the other open, still warm.
I kiss the hands that gave so much
I will see you later, my friend.

FICTION

Leave A Message After The Beep

"Hey Danny, this is Shawn. I was hoping I could catch up with you. I hate leaving a message. I'm at the Atlanta airport heading for L.A. I don't have your address. Your mom said she didn't have it, either, since you moved. This Atlanta airport is noisy and as big as a city. I missed my flight so my luggage will get there before I do. The customer service agent was apologetic and said, "Often people underestimate the size of the airport and don't allow enough time." I wanted to punch her, but I just accepted the bag she gave me. The bag contained an oversized T shirt, miniature size toiletries and a discount card for a cheap hotel. I opted to stay at the airport and sleep sitting up all night.

"I really miss you, Bro. We have had so many good times and a few bad times, too. Remember when we had a fight in middle school over that cute freckle-face Amy Johnson? Neither of us wanted to fight, so we just wrestled and rolled down the hill into the pond behind the school. You looked so funny covered in mud everywhere except one side of your blond head. You told me nothing was showing except my eyes. We laughed until our sides hurt. Then we started to decide what lie we would tell our parents about coming home so dirty. I think you came up with the biggest lie. Or was it me? I think our parents knew all about it before we got home. We vowed to be friends for life.

"When we were in college, we were worse. Sharing a beer, some grass, talking about girls and what we were going to do after college. At graduation, you signed up for the Marines. My parents sent me to Canada. It was quite an adjustment. I know it couldn't compare to the adjustment you had to make in Vietnam. Did you ever forgive me for not going with you?

"Danny, did you pick up the phone? Danny, are you there? I promise I won't keep you long."

"Did you say you wouldn't keep me long?" The voice was low and creepy. Next there was a noise that exploded in my ear. It sounded like a gun shot. Then I heard a loud thud like something heavy was dropped to the floor. I don't know if I was thinking or talking out loud. I hung up and sat back in my seat sweating profusely. How will I tell Danny's mom? How can I forgive myself for not keeping in touch? The phone rang as soon as I hung up. It was Danny!

"Hey Dude, I tried to call you right back."

"Is this you, Danny?" I was still shaking.

"Of course it's me you big idiot. You fell for my little stunt, hook, line, and sinker. Didn't mom tell you, I came out here to get an acting job?" Danny was laughing so hard he didn't hear me say, "No, I guess she didn't."

"My address is 256 Madison Street, Apartment 2. Now get yourself out here! We've got a lot of catching up to do! Oh yes, I forgive you for not going with me to join the Marines." He was still laughing.

I sat back in the well-worn airplane seat, pulled my jacket over my head and waited for the next flight.

Magazine Lovers Unite

In my house, there are stacks of magazines. Every kind of sports magazine is there; auto books on every model of car, Time Magazine and Money Magazine, just to name a few. The list could go on and on. My dear husband is obsessed with magazines. He can't get enough of them. He needs to be stopped by any means necessary! No amount of complaining, crying or cajoling seems to help.

I need help! What's a girl to do? These magazines are causing too much weight on the foundation of my house and my nerves. Surely you have learned that there are people who can help me, or at least tell me you will take a few magazines off my hands. Is there some kind of society that can help; one that's like AA? It could be called MA (Magazines Anonymous) for hoarders of magazines. Maybe I'll start it myself. I'm sure there are others out there who are suffering from this problem.

Magazine sufferers of the world let's unite and save the world from being consumed by magazines, one house at a time. Call me. I'm ready to get started. Time is of the essence. You can find me under 123 getting-ticked-off.

Before The Sun Goes Down

Before the sun had gone down, the clock struck 9:00 PM and the blind man, Benjamin, started to make his way home. He was a favorite of many customers. He stood outside the Post Office selling brooms. He loved to tell stories and he would always embellish them to the delight of all who passed or bought brooms from him.

When he did get home in the evening, there was no need to switch on the light. The grandfather clock would chime every hour. He loved the sound. Bedtime for him was usually ten o'clock, but sometimes a bit later.

Benjamin had flowers in his yard, lots of foliage. He could smell and touch them, which he loved to do on summer mornings before he began his day. It was a nice evening. Everything was quiet. It seemed hushed. Is there a storm coming? Benjamin wondered. If so, there would be no broom selling tomorrow. Oh well, there's another day. I have lots to do.

Benjamin had no fear about living alone. He had lost his sight in an explosion in Vietnam. He could protect himself quite well. He knew all the defense tactics and he had the advantage of the dark if there was an intruder.

Benjamin had many hobbies that occupied his time when there was inclement weather. One of them was his pen collection. He took great pride in his quill pen that could still be used. Benjamin also was enthusiastic about exercise and went through his routines every morning.

Benjamin was happy with his life. He had no regrets or complaints.

Thanksgiving

L et's make things easy this year. Everyone gets to eat turkey with stuffing and pumpkin pie and fall into a deep sleep after dinner, except the cook. Grandma had cooked the Thanksgiving dinner every year. No one volunteered to help. This year, grandma decided to order everything from Kroger's; the turkey, a ham, pies, cakes, and everything in between.

Grandma asked eighteen-year-old David if he would ask his twenty-one-year-old brother Don to go with him to pick up the dinner. Both procrastinated and the time for the dinner was soon approaching. The boys continued to play video games and watch football. The rest of the family, about twenty of them, was expected in an hour and no one had gone to pick up the food for dinner.

Grandma screamed at them to no avail. Nothing seemed to move them. She was angry and frustrated. What a way to spend Thanksgiving Day. She picked up a broom, turned off the television, and commenced to hit the boys with the broom. She didn't mean to say it, but it just slipped out. "Get your sorry asses up, and go to the store and pick up the food," she shouted.

The boys got up, laughing at Grandma, and went to the store. They were gone for a long time. They were so late the clerk thought they had changed their mind and sold everything Grandma had ordered to someone else. She returned the money. What could they do? The only thing they could do, I guess. They went to the nearest Chinese restaurant and bought dinners for everyone. You can bet your last dollar Grandma was not pleased.

Buttermilk Biscuits

Grandmother knew the best way to stop the incessant chatter and questions was to bake buttermilk biscuits with piles of sweet butter and rhubarb jelly. After the kid devoured three buttermilk biscuits with jelly, she started asking questions.

"Grandma, how do you make buttermilk biscuits?"

"How can you make jelly out of rhubarb? Is rhubarb a vegetable?"

"Did you notice, Grandma, the jelly is the color of a jelly bean?"

"Tell me again about the glass bowl. Where did it come from? Did you bring it from Georgia?"

"Do you have bowls any other color? If you do, may I see them?"

"Did you say they were pressed glass? How do you press glass?"

"What is carnival glass?"

"When the circus comes to town, will you take me?"

"May I have another biscuit with butter and jelly, please?"

The Grandmother sighs, wipes her hands on her homemade apron and asks, "Child, do you think your mother is home yet?"

The Ritual

Yahmi awoke before the sun shone through the cracks of the hut she shared with her husband and daughter. She had not slept well. Today is the day for the ritual. I am concerned about all the preparations. I wish my husband, Umbaka, was here, she thought. He had left with the other men of the village to hunt for food for the ritual feast. The ritual celebration is for her daughter, Bendua. She dressed quickly and called to Bendua who hadn't slept well, either.

"Wake up, Bendua. Hurry and get dressed. I must leave now to meet the other women at the end of the ritual path to help prepare for your ritual. Kenyatta will be here soon to walk with you."

"I'm not asleep. I'll be ready," Bendua said. By the time she dressed, her friend was waiting at the door of the hut.

"Good Morning, Kenyatta," Bendua said as Kenyatta presented her with flowers.

"Oh, thank you! Gold acacia and pink lotus; I love them."

Bendua and her friend, Kenyatta, talk excitedly. "I thought this day would never come," said Bendua. The girls hold hands as they walk from their tiny village near the Gold Coast of Africa. Bendua has been told many times that at the end of the path is the ritual that changes a little girl into a woman. She and Moiya, a younger friend, were caught last year spying on the old 'root woman' and the village women. They were chastised and sent back to the village. This is Bendua's day to find out about this great mystery.

"What goes on and how does it happen?" she asks Kenyatta. "The elders told me I must not tell you," Kenyatta answered. Bendua is twelve years old and it is time for her to go through this miraculous change.

Bendau is a pretty girl. Everyone in the village says so. Even the shy young man who follows her sometimes says so. Bendua's eyes are almond shaped. Her skin is dark and flawless and has a dewy look. She is small for her age. Today she is wearing her best clothes made of mud cloth. She has been given gifts of shell bracelets for her wrist and upper arms. Her mother braided her hair in rows of circles with bead intertwined. "How pretty you look," Kenyatta said. "This is your special day." Bendua hoped Kenyatta would tell her about the ritual since she is 14. But even though she pleaded, Kenyatta would tell her nothing.

They are both so excited that they don't hear the singing of the birds or the chattering of the monkeys. Nor do they pay attention to the lushness of the jungle with its date palm, acacia and mahogany trees. Neither of them remembers to be careful. It seemed to take only a few minutes to walk almost a mile to the place for the anticipated ritual. At the end of the path, Bendua can see her mother and the other women of the village waiting.

There is something she doesn't see. Shots ring out and people are running and screaming. "What is happening," Bendua shouted to Kenyatta. She could not hear her answer. Bendua and Kenyatta feel the heavy, thick, rope-like net suddenly cover them over, changing their lives forever. Bendua may never know this was the day of her female circumcision.

What Does Freedom Mean?

Cantner Fortress, Tennessee 1865

Jessie woke early. It was a warm day that wasn't unusual for Pigeon Fortress. The sun flooded her tiny room, which was not much larger than a closet. It is her room and she doesn't have to share it with anyone. No one could. There is only room for her cot, covered with colorful quilts, and two shelves which held her only dress, a few changes of underwear, and her homemade rag doll with her buttons for eyes.

The gray buttons used for the doll's eyes match Jessie's. Her skin is the color of bread crust. Her hair is like brown silk and hangs to the middle of her back. She is a beautiful child and Master Larsen cannot hide his love for her. He and his wife have no children. Jessie looks more like Master Larsen than her mother. Her mother has dark skin and she is beautiful. Her figure is lean and well proportioned, no doubt developed from her hard work in the field. Her eyes are shaped like her grandmother, Bendua.

Sometimes, Jessie is afraid to be alone in her room. Ten years old is young to be alone. Her mother, Lila, told her how fortunate she is to work and live in the "big house" and not have to work in the field.

Jessie's family is enslaved on the Larsen plantation. Master Larsen is Jessie's father; of course, he would never admit it. Mrs. Larsen knows her husband fathered Jessie, but it is something that isn't discussed. She is indifferent to Jessie. The cook mothers Jessie and instructs her in her chores. Jessie rarely sees her mother, and her mother is not allowed to go into the big house. Master Larsen often goes to Jessie mother's shack after he thinks everyone has gone to bed, and her husband is given chores in the evening.

Jessie's mother, Lila, has three older children by her husband, who is also a field hand. When he resented Master Larsen's advances toward his wife and became belligerent, he was sold to a plantation owner in Mississippi. Lila was grief stricken. The slaves heard that slaveholders were meaner further south. Lila's other children and the field hands resented Jessie and the others who worked in the big house. They felt their lives were so much easier. Often, the ones chosen to work in the big house were mulattos.

The field hands heard from people passing through that they were going to be freed. The cook told Jessie about it, but she didn't understand what freedom meant. Except for having to slip off to see her mother, whom she loved deeply, she didn't know any other way to live.

The day after the cook told her about freedom, her mother came to the kitchen door and asked Jessie to come out. Jessie was surprised; her mother had never come to the house before. Her mother said, "Master Larsen told her and the others they had been freed." He begged them to stay and said he would try to pay them. There were fifty families on the plantation and most decided to stay. They said they didn't have any place else to go. Master Larsen asked Lila to leave Jessie there. He promised he would always take care of her. Lila told Jessie she was going on ahead and would have her sister and brothers come for her in the middle of the night. She asked Jessie to leave the window open. Lila didn't believe Master Larsen would willingly let Jessie go. She also thought whoever made the decision to free them might change his mind. So, she wanted to leave as soon as possible. Jessie heard of a place where Cherokee Indians lived and they had helped many runaways. She wanted to find her husband, Jed, who had been sold off, but she was afraid to go further south.

Lila waited until the sun went down and gathered her few possessions and headed toward the Smoky Mountains with her children and a few others. As Jessie had been told, there was a tapping on her window. She had just fallen asleep and woke with a start. She picked up her bag, which contained her one dress, underwear, and her rag doll. Jessie was reluctant to go, but she loved her mother and wanted to be with her. Her

sister and brothers roughly pulled her through the open window. After
she was on the ground, they started running, almost leaving her behind.
She ran until she thought her heart would stop, and begged them to stop.
They finally did, grumbling that they had to catch up with mama and
the others who were waiting at the foot of the mountains. After what
seemed like hours, they reached mama and the others. Jessie leaped into
her mother's arms. She was so happy to see her.

The group found a place to camp, but it was cold and too damp to
make a fire. Lila and the others decided they had better keep moving.
Jessie was so tired; she fell behind the others. No one seemed to notice
when Jessie tripped on a branch and felt herself falling. She started
screaming then everything went dark. Lila heard Jessie's screams and
ran back, but could not find any trace of her. She called Jessie's name
over and over, and prayed she would find her. The other children and
adults searched until they felt it was hopeless. They agreed that Jessie
had tripped and fallen over the side of the mountain to her death. Again,
Lila grieved. Her husband was gone and her youngest child. "Why didn't
I leave her with Master Larsen?" she moaned, "If I had, I might have seen
her again." She was inconsolable, but she had to go on, and did so with
great reluctance. The clothes they wore gave little protection from the
cold of the mountains.

There was nothing else she could do. They walked all night, stopping
only for short periods of time. As the sun came up, they were leaving
the mountains. The heat of the sun felt good on their cold, tired bodies.
"Where do we go from here and what is this freedom thing going to be
like?" they asked one another.

In the distance, they saw people who they thought were coming
toward them. They had seen Indians passing the plantation. The
overseer told them they were called the Mountain Indians. Were they
friendly, or had they left the plantation to be killed by Indians? Lila and
the others were relieved to find the Indians were friendly and gave them
food and shelter. They enjoyed their hospitality for several days, then
they decided to move on. They were given food and clothing for their
journey. They were so grateful and tried in the best way they could to
express their gratitude. Lila hoped one day she could repay them. After
several days, they ended up in Georgia, a day's journey from the Indian

village. They saw a farmer working in the field and asked if he needed workers. The farmer said, "My slaves run off as soon as they heard about that Yankee law to free the slaves. If you all are willing to work hard, I will give you a plot of land to work. Lila and the others readily agreed and became sharecroppers. Maybe this is freedom Lila thought.

Jessie opened her eyes, some of the darkness started to clear. Where am I? she wondered. The pain in her body was excruciating. The smoke in the mountains was thick, but she could see that she was on a small surface of the mountain, just a few feet wider than her body. The platform of rock had kept her from falling hundreds of feet over the side. She had fallen about ten feet, but how would she ever get out. No one would ever find her there and there was no way to climb up the side of the mountain. There were no ridges for her to hold on to. She began to cry, thinking she would die there when she had had her own room at the big house. Why was freedom so important that her mama would risk her life to have it? Jessie cried harder then; she began to scream because she was in pain, cold, hungry, and afraid. She stopped screaming because she heard what sounded like someone riding a horse. She started screaming again to get the rider's attention. When she stopped and looked up, she saw a thick rope being lowered. She didn't care who was on the other end of the rope. She just wanted to get up the mountain. She grabbed the rope and held on with all the strength she had. Her arms were scratched, but within a few minutes, she was pulled to the top where she stood at the last on solid ground. The smoke obscured the figure on horseback. As the rider came closer, she gasped and nearly fainted. Sitting regally on a black horse was the most beautiful person she had ever seen. He looked to be fifteen or sixteen years old. His skin was brown with a tint of red. His hair, like Jessie's, hung halfway down his back, but was jet black and as shiny as a raven's wings. His hair was parted in the middle, with a thick braid on each side of the part. Multicolored beads adorned the braids. He wore a band with one feather in it around his head. Jessie was so awe struck she forgot her pain and her manners for a few minutes. Finally, she said, "Thank you very much. My name is Jessie." He gave her an inquisitive look and patted his chest and said, "White Feather."

He motioned for Jessie to get on the horse behind him. She gestured to let him know she didn't know how. He got down from the horse, which was covered by a colorful blanket and lifted her on to the horse. He lifted her as if she weighed very little. He sat in front of her and took her arms and placed them around his waist.

For the first time in her life, Jessie had met a Cherokee Indian. Each step the horse made was painful to her. They finally reached the camp and were surrounded by people who looked like White Feather. He said something to them she couldn't understand. He lifted her from the horse and everything got dark again. When she awoke, a woman was sitting beside her. Her arm was in a sling and her right ankle was bandaged. The woman was offering her food. She had been in so much pain that she had forgotten how hungry she was. The woman was very kind. Every day, White Feather came to see how she was feeling. He knew quite a few words that she understood. In a few weeks, Jessie was up and about. Now, there were children to play with. The woman's name was Little Flower. She treated Jessie like a daughter and taught her the ways and some of the language of her people.

She soon found out there were three white men in the camp, one named O'Dare. They were all from a place across the ocean called Ireland. Mr. O'Dare was a teacher and trader. One of the other men was a doctor and the other a blacksmith. They were all married to Cherokee women. The camp is called O'Dareville. White Feather told Jessie that there is a school and he attends every day. Jessie asked Little Flower if she could go to school. She readily agreed, so Jessie started to school with the other children. She worked hard on her studies, but a day didn't go by that she didn't think about her mother.

* * *

In the summer of 1870, Jessie was fifteen years old and had become even more beautiful. White Feather was twenty-one. He had matured, his English was almost flawless and he had learned almost everything the doctor had taught him. He learned to mix medicines, set broken limbs, deliver babies, and even determine the cause of an ailment by listening to the symptoms. The village doctor was getting older, so he passed as much of his knowledge to White Feather as possible. Jessie was now able to assist with teaching the children. They saw each other every day and it was obvious to everyone in the village that they were in love.

In the fall, White Feather asked his father and Little Flower if he could marry Jessie. Jessie was thrilled when White Feather asked her. They were married in a customary Indian ceremony. She was radiant in her white buckskin wedding dress with matching boots, adorned with beads. White Feather wore tan buckskin. They made a handsome couple.

White Feather and Jessie enjoyed many happy years together with White Feather now the doctor for the village and Jessie teaching the children. Unknown to Jessie, her mother continued to live on the farm that she and the children and other released slaves first went to after leaving Master Larsen's plantation. All of the others had moved on, looking for better jobs, including her children. She could never bring herself to move far from where she last saw Jessie. Lila's heart was beginning to deteriorate due to all the hard work she had done. The farmer, Mr. Thomas, had become quite fond of Lila over the years and did not require her to do much work. He gave her a small, well-furnished and comfortable house near his.

Lila became quite ill one day and Mr. Thomas knew she needed a doctor. The local white doctors would only treat colored people if they were not busy with their other patients. There was no doctor available and Mr. Thomas was afraid Lila would die without proper care. He had heard of a Cherokee village called O'Dareville, where there was a young Indian doctor. He decided to take her to the village for care. He lined his wagon with blankets to make Lila comfortable. She was weak and slept all the way. When he arrived at the village, he explained why they had come. White Feather knew right away that Lila had pneumonia and other physical problems that were beyond his knowledge. He told Mr. Thomas she needed constant care and he must leave her there until she recovered, if she ever did. Mr. Thomas stayed all day and reluctantly left Lila. White Feather sent for Jessie to help care for the woman. Jessie came and knew immediately it was her mother whom she had not seen in more than ten years. She was overjoyed. Jessie had told the story of the plantation and her separation from her mother to White Feather many times. He knew it well and hoped he could do something to save Lila. Lila lay feverish and drenched with sweat. After a few days, she opened her eyes and tried to focus. Standing over her, to her surprise, was a very handsome young Indian man who she didn't know. Who was holding her hand? Could it be?...No, Jessie had died in the mountains. Then, she heard Jessie say, "Mama. Mama, it's me, Jessie!" Lila thought she was dreaming, but Jessie poured out the whole story of what had happened and how wonderful her life had been, except for missing her so much. Lila began to regain some strength. She too, was overjoyed. She laughed and cried until she was exhausted.

In the days that followed, Lila grew stronger. Except for seeing her husband, Jed, and her other children, again, she felt that her life had been complete. Who knows, maybe that, too, could happen someday. She had lived to see all her children making their own way in life, even the youngest whom she had thought she lost forever. "At last," Lila said, "I think I know what this freedom thing is."

Lila lived out her remaining years with Jessie and White Feather. She was given her own hut. Jessie saw to it that her mother's needs were met. Lila never saw her husband Jed again. Jessie and White feather made her a wind chime to place at her door and a dream catcher to place over her bed. Lila died in 1885 at the age of 50.

Maybe in 200 years, Lila's descendants may know what real freedom is like.

Dry Sticks

It was a windy day; the leaves were dry. They lay singularly and together. Some leaves wanted the company of others. They wondered what would become of them. Would they be gathered up and crushed to make compost, or would they remain on the ground 'til spring to be stepped on or covered with snow?

The dry sticks from the trees became brittle and fell to the ground. The big stick had an idea. He had been thinking about it all through June. "I will just rub myself against another stick," the larger stick said.

"I don't like the idea," the smaller stick said.

"You have no choice. I am bigger than you. I don't want to hang around 'til spring." So the big stick rubbed against the smaller stick. The wind blew and soon there was a fire. The big stick was overjoyed because he thought he would go out in a blaze of glory. The fire was out of control and firefighters came from everywhere to put out the fire. No one could ever determine exactly how the fire was started.

What is the moral of the story?

I guess the big sticks sometimes take advantage of little sticks and start a lot of trouble.

A Hairy Tale

My hair has fallen asleep a lot since I now take a sleep medication. My hair goes to sleep before I do. I can feel it trying to shake each strand awake. I can hear them talking. "Wake up," the back of my head demands. I am thicker, therefore I am in charge. The top of my head replies, "I know, but I'm not as strong as you. Stay awake at least long enough to pray then listen to the weather report."

"No, I just don't care. I'm sleepy," said the thin hair at the top.

"If you don't stay awake, I'm going to tickle you 'til you giggle."

"Go ahead, do what you like. I just can't fight the sleep medication. It's stronger than you and all the hair on her head."

"I guess you're right," said the thick hair sleepily. "But, will you try a little harder to grow a bit more hair on top?"

"I always try, but it doesn't seem to happen."

"Goodnight all you strands." The hair in the middle yawns. "And try to wake up a bit more bouncy, so we don't have a hat crushed on us or be under those ugly old wigs."

"Please shut up?" said the hair in the middle of my head. "I will see you in the morning. Do not—do you hear me? Do not lose one strand tonight!"

The Knight And The King

The King woke up in his usual foul mood. Nothing pleased him these days. No one could interpret his dream. On this particular morning, there were great bolts of lighting and it rained all day. The King was convinced that this was another sign in addition to his dream. Neither the Queen nor the soothsayer could interpret his dream. So...in a fit of anger he threw them all out of the tower window.

The dream was about a hand holding a stick with a few leaves sprouting from it. The hand and stick seemed to appear from the sky. "What does it mean," the King moaned. He was furious.

Knights and countrymen from afar had heard of the King's fury and knew he would be willing to pay in gold and silver for the interpretation of the dream. A knight from the faraway country of Penacles knew that he could interpret the dream and claim silver and gold. He traveled day and night to get to the King. He brought a round globe with a star in it with him. He arrived on his beautiful horse attired in his coat of armor. He was handsome and quite striking. He asked to speak to the King and the King gave him an audience.

"What does the dream mean?" the King demanded.

The knight addressed the King and showered him with accolades. "You are the greatest King in the whole world," said the knight. Everyone from far and wide has heard of your conquests, your generosity, and your love for your subjects. The King was flattered. He was selfish, unkind, and egotistical. Flattery was the key to open the door to the King's dream, thought the handsome knight.

"How do you know all these things?" the King asked. "They are true of course," the King gloated.

The knight showed the round globe to the egotistical King and said, "Do you see this round globe? There is a star inside every way you turn it. The point of the star points to you. This shows, Oh King, that you are the star of the universe and the wisest King who ever lived." The King was pleased, rewarded the knight and started to treat his subjects with love and compassion.

The knight left in search of another greedy, egotistical king who would give him gold and silver for stroking his ego. In the end, everyone won: The egotistical King, the knight, and the subjects, who no longer lived in fear.

The Wedding

Andrea was so excited when Don asked her to marry him. They had been friends for years and grew up in the same neighborhood. Andrea and Don's parents weren't surprised at all that they wanted to get married. Everyone was pleased. There was much planning to be done – picking a dress, contacting her friends to be a part of the wedding. Don and Andrea attended the same church so, of course, they would get married there.

Three months passed and everything was done. The reception would be at the church. Andrea's mother helped her to pick a beautiful gown with lace, seed pearls, and small iridescent sequins. The train of the dress was about three feet long. Her headdress was a diamond-like tiara. Her bridesmaids were to be dressed in maroon satin, strapless dresses that were full length. The church was decorated with white roses, greenery, and netting. There were tall vases of flowers at the front of the church.

Tonight was the wedding rehearsal. Don had worked hard to get his groomsmen to wear the color jacket that would complement the bride and her bridesmaids. There was so much excitement. Andrea stood at the back of the church admiring how the church had been decorated and thinking about her beautiful dress. She would look like a princess, the way she had always known she would look at her wedding.

She felt a chill and she began to shake. She knew in spite of everything that had been done, she would never walk down that aisle. What could she say to Don, to her parents, to the bridesmaids and groomsmen who had all come from different cities? Where could she run to? Andrea quietly slipped out and went back to her apartment alone. She picked up the suitcase she had packed for her honeymoon, picked up her purse, got in her car, and headed for the airport. Where will she go? She sat in the car at the airport for a while then drove back to the church. In all the wedding excitement, she hadn't been missed.

Andrea married Don. After 20 years and two children, she is still wondering if she should've gotten on a plane, any plane, to see where life would have taken her.

First Assignment

Amy was excited about going on her first assignment. Her company was sending her to New York to open a call center. The only thing that was negative about this was Jason had to go with her.

Amy had worked her way up in the company. She had worked in sales, correspondence and auditing. She had been at Benlyn Company for twelve years. She felt that she was ready for a leadership position. Why did Jason have to tag along? The company felt that he needed the experience.

Jason was at the airport when she arrived. "Good morning," Jason said. Amy grumbled. He was too cheery for a 6:00 a.m. flight.

Jason rattled on and on. She tried to sleep in her plane seat to no avail.

Amy finally slipped off to sleep when she was suddenly shaken awake by the plane. Then she saw the flight attendant almost tossed to the middle of the plane. Cabin lights blinked on and off.

The captain said over the intercom system, "Please take your seats. We are experiencing some turbulence."

Jason started talking at first, although she was too frightened to hear what he was saying. Then she heard him say, "Hail, Mary, full of grace… be with us now and at the hour of our death."

"What is he talking about? We are not going to die," she said. It was going to be her first real assignment in New York.

The plane dropped in altitude to what felt like a few stories. She heard Jason say, "Don't be afraid. It won't be long."

"Long for what?" she asked.

Jason took her hand. She let him hold it. "It will be okay," he tried to assure her.

Then she saw it. Their plane was heading for a tall building. "It looks like we are going to hit it!" she wailed. "No, we can't, not today; no, not today. No, not today…"

She awoke with a start. How long had she been sleeping? "Damn, I missed my flight." How long did I sleep? she wondered. "The company will be furious with me. I'll call them right away. I know they will understand. I will never forget this day. I'm sure Jason went on without me. I'll write a note in my journal: '9/11, 2001, I missed my flight. I'll never do that again.'"

IN THE GARDEN

Clouds

I woke startled. My heart was beating fast. What woke me? Opening the blinds, the sky was gray. Gray isn't one of my favorite colors; however, according to the weather report, the gray sky would be replaced in the afternoon by blue skies with white clouds. I'll just get back into bed and wait till the sky is blue and full of clouds.

Cloudy days feel sad. The evergreens are not as green, the flowers not as colorful. The iridescent colors on rocks do not gleam as highly. Gray, cloudy days seem empty, void of life. Perhaps it's a state of mind. I will force my mind to see things differently.

Gray is really a beautiful color. From it, so many other colors can be blended into blues and greens. Life is about how you look at it. Deception. I won't go back to bed. I cannot afford to waste a single moment that I will never get back. Look up, it's a magnificent day! I won't be affected, whether blue or gray skies, clouds or no clouds. Don't judge a day by its weather. It's a great day to be alive!

Spring Again

It's another spring and the jonquils, tulips, and trees of white pine and bushes of red are glorious. The trees seem to bloom almost as I watch, at least overnight.

Seeing it after a long winter makes me want to sing and dance.

Just as the seasons change, so does my body, but not in a glorious way.

Almost as I watch, wrinkles appear and as much as I want to dance, my body will not do the things I long to do. So be it. But I can sing! And I will.

Who knows, maybe I will dance. Mom said you can do anything if you really want to. I'm not so sure. I think I'm going to live to 2080 when everyone will be wired and you have the ability to press a light to determine your health. A bright light will indicate wellness. A dull light would show your need to be serviced. Just like a car. I'm not worried. As I said, I plan to live to 2080. Maybe the rapture will come before then, and I'll be out of here!

Cleaning Day

It's time for spring cleaning, so I've heard. I must "spring" into action. "Tom, open the window! Why it's raining! I like the sound of the rain; it's so relaxing."

"Why are you talking about relaxing? You said it was time for spring cleaning," he says. I didn't mean really clean the house, unless we get around to it. It's a time to sit and listen to the rain and the barking dog across the street. Do you remember when he came over and sat on the porch? He's the big white dog. He escapes across the invisible fence in his yard often. I read his tag once. It said, "Not Lost, Just Wandering." He was very friendly. I patted him and released him to wander. Lucky dog!

When I sit on the porch, I don't hear children playing. They have all grown up now. No more requests for us to buy Girl Scout cookies. I miss the children and the cookies, too. I guess I'd better stop reminiscing and get some work done.

"Tom, are you looking at another ball game? Please get up and help me with the housework."

"What do you want me to do?" Tom replies in a slightly disgruntled tone.

I feel badly that I snapped at him. I'm just sitting here with a book on my lap listening to the wind chimes on the porch as the wind blows gently. "Never mind, honey; let's just take our own holiday," I said. "The housework will always be here. Did you know the rhubarb came up since yesterday?

Since I announced the holiday, Tom is back to his ball games.

The blooming tulip tree in the front yard is resplendent with pink blossoms. I know everyone who passes admires that tree. The lilac tree is about to bloom, also. I must get up and check on Rocky the Stone. He is getting covered up by the new beautiful green grass. I wonder if he minds. I had better go out and check. I wouldn't want him to be cross with me.

"How are you doing, Rocky?"

"I told her a million times, I am a stone. I am OK, thanks for asking."

It's a fantastic day," I said. "I should not waste it on spring cleaning. Just cleaning my mind of negative thoughts is enough."

Rocky responded, "I used to be sitting closer to the rosebush. I don't know what happened. One day, I found myself at least a foot from the roses and the beautiful bush and the tree. At times, I just don't like it. Why didn't someone notice that I am sitting out here away from the other stones? I think it's because I'm so special; I can see more. I can see all of the backyard, the fence, and the traffic. I know everything about the house, when it was built, who has lived in it, and often I can hear the conversation of people when they gather in the backyard. I have made friends with the birds and the squirrels. I am so glad to be away from that stuck up Rosy the rose bush. And I am not too far from Rudy Rhubarb. He's my buddy.

"Oh yes, I am special. I have so many colors and even look striped. The owner of the house admires me often from the kitchen window. I hope no one ever thinks that I should be surrounding the flowers like the other stones.

"Everyone should know that <u>I Am Special</u>!"

Another Sunny Day

The wind rustles the leaves on a tree when I am having lunch. What kind of red berries are in the tree out there? The birds seemed to like them. I must be careful when I leave. I wouldn't want my head to be the landing place for red berry bird droppings. The sky is an azure blue. There are some gray clouds. There seems to be a quiet discussion between the clouds and the sky concerning the weather for the day. It looks like the blue sky is winning over the gray clouds. Hooray, looks like another sunny day. No matter what the weather, it is a great day, and I am grateful. I think the birds think so, too.

Waiting For A Call

A day to rest is hard to come by, Anne thought. There is so much to do; dishes need to be done, washing is piling up, and the kitchen needs mopping. Well, it will all still be there tomorrow. Anne opens up the blinds and looks out at the beautiful tall green evergreen trees and Kobe, the neighbors golden retriever, is enjoying the grass and chasing squirrels. He barks Hello. I'm going outside to enjoy this beautiful day, Anne said. There will be few days left before the ground is covered with snow. She takes her cup of tea out to the screened-in porch and makes herself comfortable. She vows nothing will move her from this spot.

Anne notices a fat robin sitting on the shed. The bird cocks his head from side to side. He makes no sound. He seems to be listening and looking around. Maybe he is just sitting and enjoying this day. Anne sits and listens to many bird calls and enjoys the cloud-filled sky. She can see images of so many things in the clouds. A half hour passes and the robin is still there.

Then, there is a bird call she hadn't heard before. It seemed to be the call the robin was waiting for. Then, he flew away to join the other robins. Anne leaned back to continue drinking in the beauty of the day. Then, the telephone rang and she knew her resting time was over. Maybe I have been here waiting for the call from my family like the robin. Well, I could just ignore it, maybe not.

Peonies And Roses

There were beautiful peonies and roses on the side of my grandmother's house. I loved them. They were pink and maroon and I loved picking them. The ants loved them, too! I don't know why, perhaps it was the fragrance.

Peonies have layer upon layer of large petals and large leaves. As a child, I loved to pull the petals apart to see the inside. The flower felt smooth, soft, and dewy. I tried just a few times. I didn't want to destroy the flower, but my curiosity made me want to try to figure out what made the peonies so beautiful. The roses have thorns. I know the reason.

When my grandparents passed away, I wondered who would take care of the peonies. My mother, who loved them and loved all flowers, dug the peonies up and planted them at her house. When my mother had to leave her home to go to assisted living, I dug the peonies up and took them. The flowers were unhappy for a while.

Mystery Bush

This is the year I had our yard landscaped. Would the landscape company know what the bush was? No, they didn't.

A week ago, to my surprise, the bush had bloomed into tiny white flowers with yellow buds in the center. It is a strikingly beautiful bush and looks quite welcoming as one approaches the front door. When I looked at the bush closely, I found it was a hive for "bees." Bees covered the bush on top and inside of it. They seemed to be having a great time. The bees or birds no doubt were the "culprits" or saints responsible for the beautiful bush.

Now my dilemma is: Do I dig up the bush? Do I spray the bush to get rid of the bees? If I spray the bush, will the lovely bush die? I certainly don't want the UPS man or a visitor to get stung by bees. That would be a story.

I love all flora and fauna, but I think the bush has to go! Maybe there's some alternative. I don't know what it is yet.

There are hidden memories, I think, in that bush. I can't get rid of it before I extract the memories. I can't bring to my mind "yet" (there's that word again) what the white blossoms remind me of. It's right at the tip of my tongue. Until I do, the bush will remain beautiful and full of bees!

Warning: Be careful if you pass the bush on the way in, but do come in. Perhaps you will know what the bush is. For now, I will let the bees just be.

Two months later, the mystery is no longer a mystery. It's a beautiful weed.

An Uncommon Plant

When I think of a plant or a flower that inspires me, several come to mind. A few weeks ago, I invited 25 of my family members to my home simply for the pleasure of seeing them. Most had never been to my home. It was an enormous joy to share stories with them.

They were delighted to hear the story about the generational peony bush that blooms with splendid pink blossoms every spring. I first saw this bush beside my grandmother's house when I was a child. It grew with large pink blossoms next to the rhubarb plant. My grandmother made wonderful pies from that bush.

When my mother was a young bride she took a part of the peony bush to her home. There it stayed for years till she had to go to a health care facility. I dug it up and brought it to my home. This bush is probably more than 100 years old. It gives me great pleasure to look at the family's generational plant. I don't feel that it is solely mine.

Now I wonder how long the bush will last and if anyone else will care for it, when I'm not here.

I hope the peonies will bloom every spring and look towards the sky for many years after I'm gone.

Lord, I Wish It Would Rain

Any minute now something will happen. Weeds will grow taller. The grass will get browner. Perhaps my evergreen will show more burnt places. I will grow older. I will be hungry.

Any minute now perhaps the sky will be gray. Clouds will darken. Thunder will roll and it will rain for days! Children will run out of the house and laugh and jump in puddles of water. The whole earth will break forth with applause to see flowers bloom and the grass green again. Birds will sit behind leaves and chirp and bathe in the wonder of rain!

Rain, oh how we miss it. Any minute now, I will rejoice and smile to myself silently remembering all the wonderful times I've spent listening to the rain.

Once I had a carport and when it rained the sound of the tapping on the roof was like a call to de-stress, to rest. I loved those times.

Lord, I wish it would rain! I don't want to forget the sound and the feel of it. My umbrella, the one that has a print of the Sistine Chapel on it, is waiting with great anticipation beside me in the car. I want to open it.

If it doesn't rain soon, I'm going to open the Sistine Chapel umbrella anyway and dream about Italy and a rainy day. Oh Lord, I wish it would rain just a few drops. Please!

It's A Grand Day

In the summer, I look forward to warm, sunny days. By warm, I mean around 75 degrees. I love sitting on the screened-in porch. No worry about an attack of a bee or fly, a mosquito or any other pesky varmint. I sit and look out at the flowers. The pink iris can be exquisite. I can see trees and bushes. The blue spruce bushes, the evergreen and the giant ash tree are magnificent. The twenty-foot evergreen and tulip tree are in the front yard out of my sight, but I can feel their presence. Here, is a place to read, doze and dream. The book I am reading often falls from my hand.

The sound breaks through my solitude. I hear a voice, "I'm home," I hear my husband say. I'm glad he is home but my mood has been shattered. He wants to talk about the State Fair. I think the man thrives on heat. Doesn't he realize there is little shade at the fair?

He has tickets and he is so excited. It took all of my strength to muster up a smile. "I have four tickets and a parking pass." He was so proud of himself.

"Good," I said half-heartedly.

All I could think of was the terrible smells; the sweltering heat; the press of people; seeing the long lines of all sorts of folks buying food that was cooked in enough grease to give you a heart attack. I don't want to go! Shall I feign illness? What can I do? Please, I just want to sit on the porch like many old folks do and watch butterflies and red birds. No sweltering in the sun. No sunburn. Just let me sit and listen to nature whisper about what a grand day it is.

Wings

I sat in my favorite chair staring through the blinds. Then I saw something that I didn't understand. It was wings flapping. It looked like the wings of a very large bird. I got up very slowly and quietly. I didn't want to disturb the bird. I wanted to know what it was doing. I very gingerly opened the blinds and the sliding glass doors. The large bird didn't seem to notice the sound of cars passing by. I stood at the door and saw her perched on the fence. It was the largest bird I had ever seen. Her legs were as thick as my small finger. Was it a hawk? I wondered. I had never seen one around here. She had a wing-spread of about the span of my arms extended outward. The bird was a mixture of gray and brown and under the wings it was pure white.

The bird was pecking on the ground at something. I had to move a bit closer. Had she caught a chipmunk? What was it? She would peck at the object then fly to the fence as if to stand guard and look around. The bird was protecting whatever it was on the ground. Then I saw what it was. It was a baby bird. It was small and looked too young to fly. Had the mother pushed the baby out of the nest thinking it was time for it to make it on its own, or did some pesky chipmunk disturb the nest? I felt so sorry watching the bird swoop down and repeatedly lift the baby bird in hopes it would fly. After many failed tries the large bird picked up the baby, held and carried it away.

Where did she take it? Perhaps back to where it was born. When we are weak and incapable of making our way, are we carried on wings back to where we came from? I sure hope so.

Transitions

L ife is filled with transitions, and so it is; the changes of feeling depression and sometimes happiness. Births, deaths, friendships made and broken. Marriage with light and air and joy, and then it falls on rocky times. Family ties are sometimes broken; sometimes stronger. Places that you have been become a distant memory. The transitions that change radically are the people who come into your life who support, love, and bless you. Sometimes a song or an old memory revives some good feeling from past yesterdays. Sometimes a grandchild delights you with his or her love and makes you laugh when they don't understand old expressions like "making a mountain out of a mole hill," or something will be "old hat" for you soon. Or my god-granddaughter, Sara, saying, "Grandma P, I got an A in Calculus." Yes, life is filled with great transitions. I look forward to them and count them as blessings.

I have come to the time in my life when I don't want to waste a minute. Each spring, with its beautiful flowers pushing their way up from the earth; each summer with its heat, beautiful birds; each fall when leaves turn from green to brown, yellow and orange; and each winter with its blankets of beautiful snow with flakes of different shapes. Like a child, I will catch snowflakes on my tongue as I did so many winters ago when I was young. I wonder when will be the last season that I see and what will the final transition be like. It will no longer matter that I wanted a Ph.D., though I didn't work to get one. The only thing that will matter is…Is it well with my soul? I want to answer with a resounding, "Yes!"

MOM

Light

As I grow older, I have far more questions than answers. No time to meditate. I have often wondered what death is like.

Do you really walk into the light with a choir singing the Hallelujah Chorus as you float through the air? Or, is there an absence of light? What will the last breath be like? Will your entire life flash before your eyes? Will you see the bright lights of cities you have visited and people you have known?

I really think dying will be a fantastic experience.

When I asked mom how she felt, trying to understand, she said, "Fine, fine, fine."

So I guess I won't worry about it.

We Are All Teachers

What you have learned is not only for you, but for others. We are all teachers. Some teach life lessons that will instruct a learner either by word or by deed, or both. Many live lives that are destructive and evil. Those in their sphere of influence learn what they see and what they are taught. Learning for me has been like a lifelong journey during which I find myself thirsty for knowledge. I'm drawn to books and to people I can learn from.

My mom said, "You have two ears and one mouth. There is a purpose for that." I try to remember her words and listen and learn. I wish I could wax poetic about this subject, but I haven't had a sip of coffee yet, and so I'm not teaching or learning. Well, here's an idea. Stop and take a sip of coffee. Now, there's a great idea and a subject to write about. Maybe war mongers and peace breakers have no coffee.

That's it. I've got it. Let's send them some cappuccino or espresso coffee! Who knows the warmongers might lay down their arms and see how good a great cup of Joe makes you feel.

Believing

Religion or believing in a higher power is a good thing, I think. I love all nature and believe the origins must be the handiwork of a loving God. I was taught this way, and I have never had reason to reject this teaching. My mother saw to it that I was very carefully taught to respect everyone and everything that God created.

This has been a challenge for me. Unlike Mother, there are so many things I do not respect: war, incivility, poverty, murder, greed, laziness, and on and on and on. Of course, Mother would say, "there is a reason for these things and, of course, there is." "This, too, shall pass," she would say.

Religion often frustrates me. Turning the other cheek seems too much to bear. One offense is too much to allow another. Oh no, Mother. I truly want to be the best I can be, but sometimes I want to be rude and shout when I see so many injustices in the world.

"What the heck is going on?" I liked to ask sometimes. Of course, I can't do that. Mother you would be so disappointed in me. Sometimes, I just want to say and do whatever I please. But Mother, you would not be pleased. Most people know you passed away six years ago. I find that very strange since you talked to me this morning."

Don't worry, mom, I will try to talk less and pray more, but it is so hard. Keep reminding me, <u>please</u>!

"Be careful for nothing; but in every thing by prayer and supplication with thanksgiving let your requests be made known unto God." – Philippians 4:6 – King James Version (KJV)

The Eyes Have It

My mother has always said, "Stand up straight. Put your shoulders back, and look the person you are talking to in their eyes." I have heard thousands of times that the eyes are the windows to the soul. If so, I have looked into the souls of so many – blue, brown, green, even a person who had one blue eye and one brown. Does the two-eye color mean there is some mix-up in the soul? I have yet to see violet eyes like Elizabeth Taylor's. Have you seen any?

There have been eyes that have been unforgettable, and I feel I could look into their souls. The blue-eyed man who helped me, a three-year old desperate to read. The blue-eyed children who couldn't speak or hear, who taught me to have compassion and joy. My brown-eyed parents who loved me beyond anything I deserved. My blue-eyed grandfather who was one of the kindest, gentlest men I have ever met. The eyes of the actor Peter Lorre as he looked down at me from my bookcase. It seems that he was looking into my soul. The eyes of poets and writers whose work touches my soul.

I have found treasures too valuable to price, when I look past the eyes and try to look into the souls of everyone I meet. Often, I can see the reflection of my own soul looking back.

Uprooted

My mother and her family lived on a street named Martindale. I have just begun to wonder why the street was so named. Who was Martindale? In going to the library today, I'll find out maybe or perhaps not.

The name was changed to "Dr. Brown." I know why it was changed. Dr. Brown was the pastor of a well known Baptist church and was a close friend to Dr. Martin Luther King, Jr. Dr. King often visited Indianapolis and his friend Dr. Brown. They probably did much strategizing on Martindale at that church concerning their fight for civil rights.

I'm glad that my mother grew up on that street because there are so many memories. In my mind, I can still see the house with the willow trees in the front yard; the peonies, roses, and rhubarb around the sides of the house. Where the house once sat is a church and many of my family attend there. I'm happy about that. When I go down Dr. Brown, it will always be Martindale.

So many wonderful memories flood my mind. I am so appreciative of all that Dr. Brown did. But it will forever be etched in my mind that the street is Martindale to me.

I can't forget the multicolored peonies in my grandmother's yard. My mother uprooted some of them from her home on Martindale and took them to her new home. When it was time for my mother to go to a senior living center, I uprooted the peonies and took them to my house.

Every time I look at the beautiful pink peonies, I think of how these peonies were plucked from my grandparents' home on Martindale, to my mother's home, and then to mine. I look for them in the spring.

Peonies are great survivors. Planting those peonies were the only times that I can remember I enjoyed being in the dirt. I don't like the feel of dirt on my hands. The peony bush fills me with so many memories of childhood, family, and most of all, Mother! She loved flowers, digging around in the dirt and planting. She always said, "I miss the red dirt of Georgia," and that is another story of being uprooted, surviving, and blooming.

Bread Pudding And Sweet Potato Pie

My mother made bread pudding. It was made from leftover bread, sugar, raisins, and cinnamon. At least, that's how I think she made it. There must have been some secret ingredient that made it taste so good. Of course, there was the white sugar icing. She didn't need a recipe for anything that she cooked, so I can't pass them on. Few people cook anyway.

Oh, I must mention those sweet potato pies. She always made at least three because my brother ate a whole one at one sitting. Sara Lee has a great sweet potato pie, but she could learn a few things from my mom.

Mom was a fantastic cook. I'm sure she learned from my grandmother. I sure wish I could make bread pudding or a sweet potato pie. I must get those recipes. Maybe I'll ask my mom. I wonder if she will tell me.

Well, mom, we've talked about a lot of things. How about those recipes, please? Is there sweet potato pie in heaven?

Looking Back, Moving Forward

Church on Wednesday and three times on Sunday. Another choir rehearsal, another voice lesson. Mother soon found out piano lessons were a waste of her money. Well…she didn't find it out till that mean teacher told her.

I rebelled and didn't do any of those things again till I became an adult. Mother always had her work cut out with me. The Bible says "bring up a child in the way they should go and when they are old they won't depart from it." I suppose it's true. Years later, it was back to choir rehearsals and voice lessons. The voice lessons took me places I never thought I would ever go.

What a joyful time it was. Thanks, mom. I hope you were pleased to see your only rebellious daughter follow in "one" of the ways you wanted her to go. You gave me an unquenchable desire to not only sing but to always want to learn more, to know the back story. And you gave me the desire to sing when times are hard and when my world is at peace, at least for a while.

So I will sing whether someone is listening or not at the time when I am a great audience of one, alone in the shower! I gave one of my great performances this morning till the water got cold.

I'll think about you, mom, and I know tomorrow will be met with bravos from you.

Another Busy Day

A young man in his 30s, medium build, clean cut stopped me in the drug store. I was walking past the perfume counter on my way to check off another activity on my busy day.

"Ma'am," he said in a hushed voice. The ma'am was a question. I stopped and just said, "Yes."

There was a little girl with him. Perhaps she was nine or ten. She was a beautiful, fair-skinned, African-American beauty. She was sipping a soda from a straw, seemingly detached from what her father was saying and doing. She reminded me of one of my own granddaughters. I complimented her beauty. The young man thanked me and continued to speak.

"We have spent 161 days in a hotel. Christian people say they will help but didn't. I couldn't for some reason get a break," he said, tearfully. "I'm not asking, but begging."

He said he needed $60 and only had $6.00. I said, "I can't help you with $54." I reached for my billfold and gave him a $10 bill. "What is your name?"

"Isario," he said.

"I will pray for you," I heard myself saying. I walked away stunned from the interruption to what was a beautiful day.

Why $60? I asked myself. Was he on drugs? Did I look like an easy mark, a doting grandmother who would do anything for her grandchildren? Did I do the right thing? Should I have dug deeper and given him more? Was it my imagination that the young man looked like my grandson and the little girl like my granddaughter? Didn't all this happen between the cologne and the hair products?

I walked toward the vitamins. Two young clerks saw the strange expression on my face and asked if they could help. I told them what happened. They were apologetic.

"No, no, it's okay, thank you. Where is the fish oil, the smallest ones?"

I thanked the clerk, paid for my purchase and sat in the car for a while.

What would mother say? She passed away seven years ago, but I find myself talking to her often. "Well, Mother, what do you think?"

"It was fine, just fine, and I'm happy you found the fish oil," Mother replied.

"Be not forgetful to entertain strangers: for thereby some have entertained angels unawares." –
Hebrews 13:2 – King James Version (KJV)

The Train Ride

Two of my friends decided they wanted to do something for cancer survivors. Both had lost family members to cancer. Their idea was to have a dinner for as many cancer survivors as they knew, and a train ride from the Indianapolis Fairgrounds to Noblesville. Donations poured in from friends and companies to pay for the dinner and train ride.

This event took place yearly. The dinners were always delicious and at a different venue each year. Some groups would always volunteer to provide music and others would happily serve. The cancer survivors were the guests of honor and they were always presented with a gift.

The train ride was an absolute joy with the train conductor in his navy blue uniform and matching cap singing corny songs like "Jimmy Cracked Corn and I Don't Care." The train was noisy and more food was served.

When we arrived at our stop in Noblesville, which took about an hour, we got off and stretched and talked to all of the people that were in different compartments of the train. Then it was time to head back. Everyone was tired, too much food and excitement for our afternoon. It was evening now and the train was quiet. Some people were sleeping. I was sitting by a window. I began to doze a bit. I woke, opened my eyes and I could see a reflection in the window. It was a reflection of my mother. It seemed so real. I reached out to touch her and my hand brushed the window. I was so disappointed. I then realized that it was a reflection of me. I had become my mother. I could see her in me. I pray I got the best part, the parts that were generous, kind, giving and forgiving. I knew at this moment, I wanted to be a true reflection of my mother. I had lots of work to do.

Thoughts

Mother's birthday came and went and I forgot. Let me count how old you would have been. I think you would have been 100 years old. You told me once you wanted to live to be 100, then you changed your mind. I guess life just got too hard. Health care centers are no fun. You had a great sense of humor. It was so hard to see you lose your joy.

I miss you so much today. I remember that you always told me to "go while you can." When I would go, you didn't want me to worry about you. I always did.

I intend to live for both of us. I know you would want me to write, to read, travel, and do all the things that make me happy.

I know your years with dad were often trying. He had his issues, as we all do. Marriage is not easy. At least it hasn't been easy for me. I am going to deal with it without losing myself. I want to enjoy the time I have left. I promise you, mother, I am going to do it with all the grace I have. I will try to be loving and kind and honest about my feelings. I know you want that for me.

Lord,
Give me the right words to express my feelings. Not stilted expressions or words that the common or ordinary person can't understand, but words that touch souls. Words that bring comfort and healing, that show caring and concern. Lord, please let my life be a reflection of You. Lead me and guide me in the way that

You would have me go. I pray that my daughter will find her way to You. Lead her to someone who will help her and give her companionship. One who loves her and loves You so much more!

Amen.

Trouble

Years and years and years ago, when I was about four or five, mother used to string up a clothesline in the kitchen in the winter to dry her undies. There were no dryers then.

She asked me to look through the window and let her know when the insurance man was coming. Insurance men collected door to door back then. She wanted to hurry and get her undies down.

Trying to do the right thing, I stepped on the porch. Neighbors were passing and I said as loud as I could, "Mother, take your undies down, the insurance man will be here soon!"

When I saw mother's face, I knew I was in BIG trouble.

Now I'm much older!

Grass is getting tall. Trouble.

The ground around the house seems to be sinking. Trouble.

The frisky squirrels are making holes in the yard. Trouble.

The courtyard in front of the house needs to be power washed. Trouble.

The floors are beginning to squeak. Trouble.

Windows need to be washed. Trouble.

Stories need to be written. Trouble.

There is so much trouble but I have decided not to let it bother me too much! Those are the only things I can really control.

I guess one of these days, I might listen to the spiritual "Soon I will be done with the troubles of this world."

I will leave politics and war to others.

I could make a long list of troubles but not yet. I'll just make a list and tackle one trouble at a time. Yea, just strike one off my list!

I'll make a list…so much trouble.

She Named Him Jesse

Many years ago, a young wife and mother had one son. She named him Jesse, after his father. She knew she also wanted a daughter to complete her family. When her son was almost four years old, she was delighted to find out she was pregnant. She prayed for a girl and asked Jesse to pray for a little sister. When her daughter was born, little Jesse was convinced it was because of his prayers alone.

Like all mothers, she had plans for her children. When her arms held this new life, she began to store up dreams that she hoped would find fulfillment in her baby girl. The dreams were as much for herself as for the daughter she held.

As she looked down at her baby daughter, she noticed her baby's eyes looked strange. She thought her child might be blind. She took her child to the hospital. The doctors confirmed her fear.

She had been taught the power of prayer, so she prayed for her baby daughter for whom she wanted so much. She named her after a poetess and writer. Perhaps she hoped this would give her daughter something to aspire to.

She took her baby to her mother. She knew her mother would know what to do through the power of prayer. Her mother assured her that her child would not remain blind, regardless of what the learned doctors said.

Her mother mixed one of her potions (something she had learned from her mother) and placed the mixture on the eyes of the child. Little Jesse held his sister's hand as often as possible. Then they prayed together and asked God to allow the child to see. They asked God for grace and mercy.

Did God answer their prayer? Did her daughter write poetry as the young mother hoped? Well, a little. Did she become a writer? Well, yes, a little! Did God give the child sight? Yes!

I was that child. I once was blind but now I see. I have been many places. I have seen many things. Now I am privileged to see your beautiful faces.

For Jesse and me that was the spring of our lives. Now we are in the winter of our lives. Jesse is now legally blind and I will hold his hand as often as I can.

My brother and I will not forget the prayers of our mother and grandmother and we will always share the love that they gave us.

Peonies And Wind Chimes

Today, mother is leaving the home where she has lived since I was five years old. Here, she lived with my father, my brother, and me. She had babysat with her grandchildren here. She loved and nourished us all. Memories are everywhere today. The wine-colored sectional sofa with the custom-made plastic covers, the mahogany dining room table with matching cabinet where lace curtains were stored is here. There's the kitchen – where I can still smell the fried apple pies and taste the bread pudding – table and chairs with chrome legs and the refrigerator that was surely too large to go through the door. All must be left behind. She was taking only her bedroom suite and boxes full of memories. My heart ached for her and myself. I knew that this was one of the most difficult days she had ever faced, except for the passing of my father, her parents, her brothers, and sisters. It's like a new death today to leave so much behind. I know she is thinking of things that transpired in every room. Especially the bedroom, where she felt my father would come and sit on his side of the bed after he passed away and stay 'til she fell asleep. She would remember, as I do, sitting on the glider on the front porch entertaining friends. I forgot to tell her the pain it brought me to leave the catalpa tree where my brother and I had a tree house as children so many years ago.

Mother loved to work in the yard. The yard was always resplendent with flowers of all kinds. There were flowers that are not as popular today. There were flowers called rooster combs (I don't know why). They were a red color and feel like velvet. There were plants called hens and chickens and dusty millers. She didn't know how these plants got their names. There were marigolds, zinnias, lily of the valleys, ferns, mints, and glorious white, pink, and maroon peonies.

Mother can't have flowers where she is moving. She is moving into an apartment for seniors because she is no longer able to care for her yard and flowers. She is now in her late eighties. To cheer her, I bought her a new colorful sofa bed, so she could have her grandchildren, whom she loved so much, stay over sometimes in her apartment. Her apartment is cozy. It has a living/dining room combination, a galley-type kitchen, one bedroom and a bathroom. Thank goodness there are two large closets because mother has so many clothes and other things she will never give up. The dining room table and chairs I bought seemed to make her happy. I feigned happiness over her new apartment. She had friends in the building and there was a grocery and laundromat there so she didn't have to leave the building if she didn't want to. The church bus would pick her up so she could continue going to church. She continued to catch the bus and do volunteer work at the Catholic Church. Mother is a life-long Baptist, but denomination meant nothing to her. She worked where she was needed. She called it her job and worked at it like she was being paid. Volunteering gave meaning to her life and great joy. She checked on her friends in the building who might be ill and always sent greeting cards for all occasions.

Mother's grandson had agreed to buy the old house, which was badly in need of repairs, and agreed to never sell it as long as she lived. After mother was settled in her apartment, I went over to the old house and dug up a small part of the enormous peony bush. I planted it in my backyard hoping it would not miss the soil of the old homestead and would bloom for me. The first year, it didn't bloom, but the second year it was beautiful with full white and pink blossoms. I was thrilled to pick them and take them to mother and tell her where I had gotten them. She was very pleased and I think perhaps a little sad, too, because the memories kept rushing back.

Mother lived in the apartment for three years and seemed to adjust very well. I visited often and she loved to cook Sunday dinner for me. I enjoyed it because I didn't want her to eat dinner alone. Since I was single, I didn't want to eat alone, either, and I really preferred to spend the time with her and listen to her stories about me and my brother, her family, and her birthplace in Homer, Georgia, Banks County. I never tired of hearing them. She never tired of telling me the stories.

Mother seemed to adjust to her new life and apartment 'til the building was changed from seniors only to people of all ages. The change was blatant. I could not only see a change in the building, but a change in mother. When I went to visit her, I could see young men hanging around cars outside, trash around the building, and the smell of marijuana in the hall. I was becoming afraid for her safety and I think she was, too, though she would never admit it. I prayed constantly that God would send angels to watch over my mother. One day, mother called and said, "I had a very strange experience last night."

"What happened?" I asked.

She said, "I didn't think I was asleep, I just had my eyes closed. When I opened my eyes there was a bright light and standing beside me was a beautiful figure surrounded by a bright light. I couldn't make out the facial features, but I know the person was beautiful. The figure was holding what looked like a writing pad and was recording something. Then the figure and the light disappeared."

I didn't want mother to be frightened, so I told her not to be afraid and I told her about my prayer and God had indeed sent an angel to watch over her. She was so happy about this she told all of her friends. Not too long after this mother said, "The angel paid another visit." I was glad because my father no longer came to sit on the side of the bed 'til she fell asleep. Perhaps he didn't feel that the apartment was his home.

The situation at the once pleasant senior facility worsened. I knew I had to find another apartment for mother. I wrote a detailed letter to another facility that was much nicer and was for seniors only. I was overjoyed that she could move in so quickly. This apartment had a balcony where she could put her plants. The size of the apartment was about the same, but there was a beautiful view of trees. She was on the third floor and each floor had a different color with a table and silk flowers to greet you as you stepped off the elevator. The foyer was lovely with sofas and easy chairs, so the residents didn't have to stay in their apartments. They also had a dining room and served lunch. The church bus still picked her up and she continued to volunteer. My worries were over, or were they?

Well, it was time for another move. My church had built a senior living facility. It was directly across the parking lot from the church and about five or six minutes from my home. Now, I knew things were looking up because I could get to her in just a few minutes. Just as I did every time she moved, I stayed overnight and slept on the couch to make sure she felt comfortable. I was glad I had started to record the stories she told me because I felt it was now too late. Mother had become delusional and her body was weakening. Through it all, she had not lost her sense of humor. She often told me things that made me laugh 'til I cried. She loved that. She told me, "I got in the bathtub instead of taking a shower. It took me two hours to get out. I promised the Lord, if I ever got out I would never get in a bathtub again."

It wasn't what she said most of the time, but the expressive way that she said it. She was still independent and wanted to do things for herself. I tried not to crush her independent spirit, but it was so hard. I wanted to do everything for her, but I watched her struggle just to get out of her Lazy Boy chair that one of her granddaughters so lovingly gave her. I would watch 'til I could no longer stand it, and I helped her to the detriment of my back. I wondered how she felt when I was learning to walk at nine months and wanted to do it myself.

Mother still was able to get around with the use of her cane. She did occasionally attend Bible class at the facility, but she still didn't socialize much. I tried to assure her that the voices she heard at the old apartment she moved from would not be heard at this apartment. It seemed for a while that she believed me. Soon, she was hearing the voices again. She said it was a man and two women who talked to her. She said they tormented her night and day trying to tell her what to do. Nothing I said could change her mind. I told her don't be frightened, just make them your friends. She didn't care for this idea. I guess that the people in her head were people she didn't want to be friendly with. I asked her how they found her since she moved. She smiled and said they just knew and they flew over. We both laughed. When I got home, I cried. I knew I was losing her.

The manager of the apartment called me on several occasions and asked me if mother had doctors' appointments. When I asked why, he said that was what mother had told him, and she was dressed nicely and was waiting for someone to pick her up. I left home immediately and assured her that she hadn't missed her appointment. This happened often. I would take her back upstairs and stay with her awhile. I asked one of the residents to look in on her, which she was glad to do. Even with the neighbor, the manager and going over to her place almost every day, I still constantly worried. Was she taking her medicine at the right time? Was she taking it at all?

Today, I decided to go to see mother. I had a key, so I let myself in. She was bending over and she said, "I can't straighten up." She was amused by it. I got a high stool and had her sit down. I called 911. It seemed like just a few minutes, and the ambulance arrived to take her to the hospital. Mother was taught to use a walker and she was on oxygen. She was there for about thirty days while they evaluated whether or not that she was capable of living alone. I was not surprised to find out that she needed 24-hour care. I took her home with me for a while, but had a two-story house and I was afraid she would fall. Making the decision to place mother in a health care center was one of the hardest things I have ever done. I visited a number of them and finally decided on one where I knew the administrator. I felt certain she would get good care there. It struck me that her home was getting smaller along with possessions. Now, her home was just a room.

We were able to bring her dresser, mirror and television set. After she was settled in her room, after leaving her home and three apartments, she asked, "Am I going to die here?" I said, "I don't know." The question broke my heart. Mother adjusted as she always seemed to do. She used her walker to go down to the dining room for some meals. Every time I came, she would say, "What did you bring me?" I never went empty handed. She would say, "Have a seat, stay a week, but don't ask for anything to eat." She would laugh heartily and so would I.

She loved visits from family, friends, and the children from the church across the street, who adopted her as their grandmother. They often wrote her letters and brought her gifts. She loved looking out of the window to see who was driving up. After a year or so, mother's body and mind started to deteriorate. The voices she heard still plagued her. One day, one of the voices told her that I had a terrible accident and was in serious condition. One of the nurses called to ask if I was all right. She told me what mother said, so I called her on the phone and told her that I was fine.

Sometimes talking on the phone was a problem because her hearing was so poor. I went over to assure her that I was fine. I told her to try to ignore the voices when they told her bad things. She said the female voice was the worst one. I told her to "Just tell her to take a hike." Mother laughed.

Mother then preferred to stay in her room and eat her meals there. I really wanted her to get out more, but she preferred to be alone. She had two roommates in the time she was there. Both passed away and she missed both of them. One day, her grandson came by and, of course, brought her some sweets. He said, "Grandmother, I am going to Europe, and I'll be gone for a few weeks. Are there people still talking to you?" he asked.

"They are still bothering me," she replied.

"Well, when I leave I am going to take them with me and they can go bother someone else in another health care center," he said with a mischievous gleam in his eyes. Mother thought about it for a moment and said, "They'll be back!" Her grandson sent a card from England and told her that the people she heard in her head were with him. She didn't believe it, but reading the card to her made her smile. Anything that makes mother smile made my day. She watched television, most often the news, The Price is Right, and her pastor just as she always did.

I had finally finished my book *Wind Chimes and Promises*. I promised mother that I would finish it. To keep me on task, she asked if I was going to complete it before she died. So, I finished it in November 2002, long before I intended to. When I finally placed the book in her hands, she asked, "Did I say all this?"

"Yes, and much more," I replied. I had a poster made of the cover of the book and placed it on her bathroom door, so she could always see it. A friend made a pillow with the cover of the book on it so she could have it on her bed. When I read some of the stories to her, she started to recall more. As she said, she could remember in vivid detail things that happened over fifty years ago, but could not remember what she had for lunch one day. I asked her what she had for lunch one day. She said, "I can't remember, but whatever it was, I didn't appreciate it!"

When mother wasn't holding court with visitors, she watched the people going back and forth down the hall. She often had funny comments about them. She started watching a lady across the hall and commented on her walking back and forth all day. She said sometimes she would come into her room, mumble something and then leave.

I tried not to tell mother when someone passed away, but she seemed to find out anyway. I guess she had inherited that trait from her mother, Sally.

In June 2001, my girlfriend Pat called, as she often did, and said she planned to be in Indianapolis that month. Pat lives in El Paso, Texas. We have been friends for many years and when she comes to town, we always have lunch. She told me her brother was coming with her and she wanted me to meet him. He lives in San Diego, California. I thought, Oh no, here we go again, somebody trying to fix me up with a relative. I had been single for 24 years and I was doing just fine.

Thank you very much! It took a number of years adjusting to being single after almost twenty years of marriage. I spent a lot of time trying to find purpose and truth, and regain my self-esteem, if I ever had it. My emotions, when it came to matters of the heart, were fragile.

I did agree to meet Pat's brother. We met at a local restaurant/deli. When I arrived, I saw an attractive man standing on the outside of the restaurant talking on a cell phone. I walked into the restaurant and greeted Pat. I didn't see anyone with her, so I thought he might feel the same way I did and decided not to come. "It's so good to see you," I said.

"It's good to see you, too, honey. Did you see my brother when you came in? He went outside to get better reception on his phone."

"Oh yes," I said enthusiastically. I was delighted. Something must be wrong with him, I thought. He walked in and Pat introduced me. There is something special about this man, I thought. We all talked for about an hour and I told them I had another appointment and must leave. Tom asked if he could call me. "I already have your number," he said with a smile. Tom and Pat were taking a vacation together to visit friends and relatives from California to Florida.

Tom, true to his word, did indeed call. He called every day from every state they visited. He continued calling after the vacation every day. After four months of daily calls, we both decided we wanted to spend some time together. I first decided I would visit him in San Diego with a friend, but changed my mind. Tom is a widower. He was in the Navy for thirty years and after retirement decided to stay in the beautiful city of San Diego. Who could blame him? I just wasn't sure a long distance relationship could work.

Tom decided to come to Indianapolis in October. I promised him I would try to hold the beautiful leaves 'til he arrived. It had been many years since he had seen the fall of the year in Indiana. He was born in Marion, Indiana and said he didn't miss Indiana winters and would not be anywhere cold on purpose. He said, now I have purpose. When Tom arrived in Indianapolis, there were only a few colorful leaves left on the trees. We had a wonderful time going out to dinner, seeing movies, and talking. It was good to have him here. It felt strange to date again. One of the first things I did was take him to the health care center to meet mother. Mother fell in love with Tom before I did. It was as though she had known him forever. She loved talking to him. Tom was so kind to her and treated her as if she was his mother. He never complained when I told him I had to go see mother every day. Of course, I took him to church, which he enjoyed very much. As hard as I tried, I couldn't find anything wrong with this man. Lord knows, I really tried. After three weeks, Tom returned to San Diego. We continued to talk every day, sometimes twice a day. In February, we decided to meet at his sister's in El Paso, Texas. I knew our relationship was getting serious, so I told him as long as my mother lived I would never leave her. He said he understood, so I thought there could be no thought of marriage. To my surprise, Tom asked me to marry him and said it didn't matter where he lived as long as he was with me. Of course, I told him I would marry him. Tom wanted to call all my friends in Indianapolis and tell them, but it was late. I was so shocked that he asked me. I told him to write it down. He did. Here is his proposal:

Phyllis Darling,

You're a very special person.
You're intelligent, caring, loving person.
I love being with you and

talking and laughing with you
and telling you how much I love you.
I will do everything earthly possible
to pamper you - make you happy
and wonderfully "alive."
I'd like to spend the rest of my
life with you. Will you marry me?

Tom
I'm Always and Forever Yours.

I flew back to Indianapolis in February. I told mother I was getting married. She said, "Are you marrying Tommy?" She remembered! When I said yes, her eyes lit up and she said, "That's fine; that's just fine! Where is he? I want to see him." I told her he would be in Indianapolis soon and he would be coming to see her. She forgot the voices she heard for a while and asked every day, "When is Tommy going to be here?" Every day, I would say soon.

At last, Tom did arrive and to say I was glad to see him would truly be an understatement. I knew God was in the plan. One of the first things we did was go to see mother. She was delighted to see him. He greeted her as he always did, with a kiss. She said, as she usually did, "Have a seat. It doesn't cost anymore to sit down." We pulled our chairs close to her bed. Mother rarely got out of her bed now. Tom pulled his chair up close and took mother's hand. "May I marry your daughter?" he asked.

She thought for a while then said, "Are you going to take good care of her? I do believe you love her, so yes, you can marry her." I couldn't believe my mother was giving permission for her daughter in her sixties to get married.

Next, we went to our pastor for counseling. We wanted to make sure we did things in a Godly way, so we married in church in the presence of about ten family members and friends. When we told mother we were married, it seemed to escape her memory that we had not always been married.

After a few months, Tom left to go to San Diego for his granddaughter's high school graduation. I agreed to join him there in a few weeks. His house had been put up for sale and we needed to clean the house. It was a wrenching experience to see Tom give all of the possessions he acquired over a lifetime away. He gave away everything except two boxes of clothes that were mailed to our home in Indianapolis. He packed boxes in his car and we shipped the car also. It was very emotional for me to know this man loved me enough to give up practically everything he had and come to a city where he knew few people and where the weather can be erratic. He has never shown any regret. God is good.

On The Way To Cedine

T he time I have waited for has finally arrived. I'm on my way to
Cedine along with twenty eight other ladies. Cedine is a Bible
and Conference Center in Spring City, Tennessee. Spring City
is east of Nashville. Retreats are held there for ladies, men, teens, and
couples. The name Cedine is a combination of the words Cedar and
Pine, which are found in great abundance on the grounds. Excitement
was high as we boarded the bus. We were headed for a weekend of
peace and tranquility, hiking, boating, horseback riding, seminars,
workshops, and bonding.

It was a beautiful day. As we rode through Kentucky and entered
Tennessee, for some reason my thoughts turned to Homer, Georgia,
Banks County, my mother's birth place. I wondered if the train that
mother and the family rode on going north to Indianapolis might have
passed this way. I could see the train tracks near the highway. Was she
full of anticipation or was she sad about leaving the only home she had
ever known? I could see the red dirt that my mother spoke of so often.
Why hadn't I ever noticed it before? I thanked God for the day, and for
my family's successful flight from the Ku Klux Klan and Georgia almost
80 years ago. I dozed off to sleep. After a few hours, I was awakened by
the excited chatter of twenty eight ladies all talking at once about their
past experiences at Cedine. This was my third trip. I looked forward
to seeing the missionaries who give of themselves so unselfishly. A
weekend of fun and relaxation and sharing for us is a weekend of hard
work for them.

I was talked into going to Cedine four years earlier by a friend. I
was filled with apprehension. I had thoughts of sleeping on a cot, taking
cold showers, walking to an outhouse and being attacked by a giant

mosquito, not to mention the possibility of seeing snakes and bears. None of this happened. The rooms accommodated three people. The beds were comfortable, and there was adequate space for moving around. There were three beds with clean linens, a desk, chairs, a bathroom with a sink, dressing table, and a shower with plenty of hot water. Through the window, you could see the beauty of the woods. There were no TVs, radios, or newspapers. No locks on the doors and none were missed.

After unpacking, we went down the hill about a quarter of a mile to the Dining Hall. There's something about being in the hills of Tennessee that makes you hungry. It's always exciting to meet ladies from North Carolina, Missouri, Kansas, Arkansas, and Georgia. As we stood in the buffet line waiting our turn to partake of the delicious food so lovingly prepared for us, it was time to socialize and exchange stories about the trip there. Ironically, I was surrounded by ladies from Georgia. Of course, I asked each one had they ever heard of Homer, Georgia, Banks County. I was disappointed that none of them had. After a delicious dinner, it was time to walk back up the hill to the Assembly Hall for announcements, introductions, ice breakers, singing, and a seminar. After a fun evening, we returned to our rooms ready for 11 PM, when the lights went off.

The following morning, our day began at 6:30 AM with a breakfast, then on to the morning seminars and workshop. The group leader kept things interesting and lively discussing women's issues. There was sometimes laughter and sometimes tears. It seemed as though time had taken flight and it was time to go back down the hill again for lunch. After lunch, we had our choice of activities. Some ladies worked on crafts. Others went hiking, horseback riding, touring on a covered wagon, or paddle boating. Some opted to take a nap. I decided to sit by a fence on a hill. I could see the mountains covered with trees, which were orange, green, and red, a myriad of colors that touched an azure sky. Sprinkled over the landscape were trees that looked like perfect Christmas trees. I imagined how they would look with snow glimmering like diamonds on the tips of their branches.

I could see in the distance Watts Bar Lake. There were tiny little islands in the middle of it. It looked like nature had made them for the birds to rest on. I also could see the white sails of boats on the lake. I heard crickets, and the songs of birds; they sounded sweeter and happier at Cedine. Perhaps, I hadn't taken time to listen at home. I don't know why, but there in Tennessee it was like the Hoagy Carmichael and Stuart Gorrell song, "Georgia On My Mind". Is this the way it is there? I was starting to feel guilty because I had found the perfect spot away from everybody. I got up, dusted off my blue jeans and took a walk. As I walked, I kicked the stones and the red dirt along the path and thought how wonderful the place was. I could feel a breeze; there was a faint smell of hay and horses. What a perfect day!

I went back to my room and read for awhile. I didn't believe it. It was time to shower and dress and start back down the hill again for dinner. Again, I was surrounded by ladies from Georgia. They were from Decatur, Elletsville, Brunswick, and other places that I had never heard of. I thought I would ask one last time at the risk of boring my roommates. "Have you ever heard of Homer, Georgia, Banks County?"

With no hesitation, one of the ladies said, "Yes, I've been through there many times." My joy had no bounds! I have never met anyone other than my mother's family who had ever heard of Homer, Georgia. She said she remembered because she always had to slow down to 35 miles an hour to go through the town. There was only one stop light and they were notorious for ticketing speeders. It was like receiving an unexpected gift. There was Homer, Georgia, Banks County, and it was five and a half hours away she told me. It was difficult to think of anything else. After dinner, it was back up the hill for part two of the seminar and a "singsperation."

Tomorrow, it would be time to say good-bye to our new friends. The time at Cedine was always too short. I left with memories of a peaceful time. Was the south in my blood passed on to me by my mother?

Leaving was difficult, remembering that I had been told Homer, Georgia was only five and a half hours away. I just knew that I would return to Cedine, and that I would see Homer, Georgia someday. We boarded the bus with our box lunches and fond memories. We were on our way back home to families, jobs, and responsibilities. The mood was jovial. There was singing and lots of talking. We had all become closer at Cedine.

A few hours later, it was quiet. Everyone was meditating or asleep. I awoke just before we arrived in Indianapolis and remembered my mother saying as she and her family approached the city from the south, she was thrilled to see the lights of Indianapolis. So was I!

Mother Did It Again

"Phyllis, come here. Is your underwear clean?

"Of course it is clean, mother. I would never go around with dirty underwear," I said indignantly. I was 30 years old.

"Well, you never know when you might be in an accident and you have to go to the hospital.

I always remembered her words, so my underwear is always clean.

It was a beautiful summer day in June. I love the month of June. I was driving my silver sports car. I was single and free and the world was full of adventure and I intended to find it.

In an instant, I felt the world spin and then I felt a blow to the car. My car ended up on the other side of the street and I couldn't focus for a moment. I don't believe that we had seat belts then. The stick shift in the floor was the only thing that had kept me from going through the open window of the car. My radio was still blaring.

I heard an unfamiliar voice say, "Are you hurt?"

"I don't know," I answered groggily. In the back of my mind, I could hear my mother's voice saying, "Make sure your underwear is clean." I heard another voice say, "Call an ambulance."

It seemed like a few minutes and I was on a gurney at the hospital. The doctor said, "It looks like you're okay, no broken bones just bruises."

I immediately called my mother and told her that I was in the hospital and I had been in a car accident. Before she could say it, I said, "Yes, mother, my underwear is clean." My mother truly believed that cleanliness is next to godliness. I still hear her voice from time to time telling me about life. Today I heard her say, "Phyllis, make sure you rake those old leaves off of the flower beds and make sure you get some rest and take your vitamins."

"Yes, mother. Please, no more instructions for today."

"One more thing," she said. "Open the windows and let the spring air in."

"OK, mother. I think that's quite enough for today."

Being Under The Catalpa Tree

From the time that I was able to walk until my teen age years, I enjoyed sitting under the Catalpa tree in the backyard.

The branches of the tree practically covered the entire back yard. In the spring, there were white blossoms and long thin green pods that looked like cigars. My father made a ladder by nailing pieces of wood just large enough to place my feet on to climb the tree. If the branches hadn't been there, I would have been able to see all over the neighborhood.

Dad did this for me because my brother, who was older than me, built a little house in the tree for him and his friends and told me, "No girls allowed." I showed my brother otherwise. I was in the tree house with my dolls every chance I got.

As I got older, just sitting under the old tree was enough. It was a time to remember the past and look forward to the future.

When I need to slow down, meditate and think about what the future holds, my mind goes back to the old tree and I think of the times so long ago when my brother thought (or maybe not) that he could keep a bratty little sister out with a sign that said "For Boys Only!"

I know that he didn't really mean it. We had picked too many small, red tomatoes together from the garden and stolen salt from the salt sprinkler, and salted the tomatoes under the tree to believe it. He always had time then and now for his sister.

When

When did I become the adult mother? And when did you become the child? Why do I have to make the decisions for both of us? I am exhausted. My mind, heart and soul are overwhelmed with thoughts, decisions and prayers.

How can I keep you with me? How can I let you go? What will I do without you?

I can hear you say so sweetly, "Will I always be with you?"

I know. I know. Of course you will.

If you must go, go with God! It is spring. This is your time! I will remember you always, but especially in the spring. This spring, mother, all the earth will bring forth beautiful flowers and the trees send their love. The roses send you a kiss; so do I. The forsythia sends their love, too.

I WAS JUST
THINKING

Home Is Home

I have a loving sweet husband, God bless him, but why in the heck can't he pick his clothes up? He doesn't mind clutter. I think he thrives on it. I, on the other hand, like things neat. Everything should be in its place. "Where's this; Where's that?" he asks every time he can't find something. I can't say anything to change him. He very sweetly apologizes and an hour later, I'm picking up his shoes from under the coffee table.

We were sitting in a restaurant with friends one afternoon and my husband said, "Did you see that SUV? It had a plate on it that looked like he might be one of the Colts." How can you look out the window and see a SUV going by at about 35 miles an hour and you can't see your socks in the middle of the floor? I would be ready for a psychiatric ward if he weren't so kind and sweet. He does the laundry and I am grateful, but he doesn't know to put anything away. It's the same way with grocery shopping. If there is a 20% sale or a "buy one, get one free" he is on it. And, he knows all the scores for every game played.

God help me, I don't know where to put all the groceries. There are shelves in the garage full of canned goods. I could jump up and down or roll on the floor and throw a tantrum, but he would just say, "Are you through yet?" I wish I had a scream room. What's a girl to do? I want an argument. I want a debate. I want a heated discussion. I won't get it at home. I don't have a dog to kick or kids at home to take it out on. I just have to hold it in 'til some snippy salesclerk, or someone asks me if I can "hold" as soon as they pick up the phone. It ticks me off! There are so many things that I'm annoyed about. I need to write a letter to "Let It Out" in the newspaper.

I'd write about: socks on the floor, crooked politicians, too many groceries, friends passing away, the cable bill and talking to one telephone answering recording after another.

It's getting on my last nerve. I am almost to the point that I want to raise the window and say, "I'm mad as hell and I'm not going to take it anymore."

This is a warning! Do not push my buttons today.

If you do, I promise that you will be sorry.

Trust

Many years ago Grandma had two insurance men who collected every week. Just inside the door, she placed a beautiful velvet holder which held two pockets. The bag was nailed to the wall. In the two pockets of the bag she placed her insurance policy books along with the money to pay each insurance man.

Once a week, the insurance men would step inside the door record the payment and take the money for that week. They would call out a thank you to Grandma who was always cooking. She would call back, "God bless you."

There was never a problem. Grandma trusted them. The insurance men trusted Grandma and they trusted each other.

As a child I never understood that kind of trust. I still don't. Grandma always said, "You never know who will take the last pillow from under your head." There is no doubt that whoever did so loved her and held her in high esteem.

It was often said that Grandma was part Native American. I don't know for sure. I can remember waist-long braids that she was able to fashion into what looked like a crown.

I don't know anyone who trusted like Grandma. She was compassionate, sweet, and serene. Today that kind of trust would probably be abused. I long for the times when trust was easier. I don't think we will ever see those times again!

Intuition

Old Mrs. Watson, who lived down the street, was so nosy I think that she never slept. She was so busy trying to meddle in everyone's business. She had no trouble repeating what she heard or surmised. I can hear her now!

"Honey, I think I ought to tell you that Henry is having an affair since he's your cousin and all. I think you ought to tell his wife!"

"You found out, Mrs. Watson. Why don't you tell his wife?"

"Well, I just don't want to get involved," Mrs. Watson said, with a wink. Getting involved was her specialty.

Mrs. Watson loved to gossip and when she was asked if what she said was factual, she would always reply, "I have intuition, you know." Mrs. Watson was the town gossip and everyone knew it. She had often been put in her place. She didn't seem to mind when she was caught spreading gossip. When that happened, she would cry and say "the spirit" told her these things.

What spirit was that? Everyone wondered. I didn't know that there was a spirit of nosiness.

She would just pull her shawl around her shoulders and take her chunky, Lily Of The Valley-perfumed self to spread more gossip. Well, God bless her. I guess being a widow and having no children she had nothing to do.

However, she did provide a laugh sometimes when embellishing a story. Who knows, maybe intuition through the spirit may have told her things.

On second thought, I don't think so.

Ups And Downs

alling, getting up and falling again, time after time, ailment after ailment. Patching up, gathering up, going up!

Life can fall apart only temporarily. Then you pull things together again, hopefully.

Mix up, get up, gather up, upstairs, up and out. Then there are the downs. Break down, going down, downstairs, down in the mouth, Down Syndrome, downward spiral. Sometimes it seems more downs than ups. Relationships up and down, things falling apart, and the ups and downs are the cycle of life; far too many to mention, few constants. Bodies, as beautifully as they are made, will fall apart. Houses will fall apart. Cars will fall apart. Only things created by God will endure forever! (Did I mean that?) Yes.

Shoes Tell A Story

I think shoes define the progression and stages of life.

When babies outgrew their first pair of shoes, they were often bronzed. At least that is what I did with my daughter's first shoes. Today they are a constant reminder that my baby is now a "woman," self-willed, intelligent, well-spoken, and self-reliant. I keep her first shoes on a dresser, the dresser that was a gift to her on her sixteenth birthday.

Every time I go into the room where the shoes are, they seem to ask the same question, "Where is the baby who wore these shoes? What is she like now?" I try to think of all that she has accomplished and I tell the shoes and they are proud. I would never tell the shoes everything about the one who wore the shoes. I think they might lose a bit of their glow.

The bronzed shoes would like to know about the red tennis shoes she loved so much that she slept in them when she was seven; the first high heels she struggled in when she was fifteen; the boots she wore at twenty-one in summer and winter because she wanted to make a statement. She is still making a statement in the shoes she wears.

I will continue to tell the shoes all the good things about the woman who once wore the baby shoes. I think that it will always make the baby shoes glow with pride.

Labels And Boxes

Have you ever bought pillows with a label that said, "Do Not Remove This Tag"? I've asked, "Why not?" After all, they were my pillows. I didn't understand it. I cut the tag off.

It seems that there are labels everywhere. We might do well to follow the instructions in some cases. Once, I washed a blouse and it came out about 5 sizes smaller. I read the label and it said "Dry clean only". I read labels now.

Labels I despise are the labels that people put on others. Like the child is slow or he is lazy, based upon little information. Another one is, "She thinks that she's important." The other labels I detest are the boxes people put you in when they meet you. The conversation goes something like this:

"What do you do?" This means that they are fishing for the label and the box.

I smile and say, "As little as possible."

They smile and say, "I mean, where do you work?"

"Where did you go to school?"

"Where did you grow up?"

"Do you know...?"

They mention someone that they think is important to see if you know him or her. If you answer these questions, you have just been labeled and put in a box of their choosing.

Be careful, watch the labels if you think that the person asking has put you in a highly favorable box with a beautiful label. You might start to believe you are who they think you are. Wear your own label and keep it securely where it belongs. No one needs to see it, except when you choose to show it. If they ask are you a believer in Christ, happily say yes and tell them why.

Did You Say South Carolina?

It's 11:30 PM and I'm jarred awake by the phone ringing. Should I answer it or just turn over and try to go back to sleep? I guess I had better answer. It might be important. If it's a wrong number, I'm going to make them sorry that they dialed my number. "Hello," I say, trying to sound as sleepy as I can. I want the caller to feel guilty for calling so late and waking me.

"Phyllis, are you asleep?" the caller asks. What an asinine question. What the blue blazes do they expect at this time of night? Doesn't she know I have to go to work tomorrow?

"Wake up for a minute. Have I got a deal for you! Are you awake?"

"Unfortunately, yes. Why are you calling me so late? You're retired. I'm not." I raise up to look at the clock. This is characteristic of my friend, Anita. I love her, but sometimes I think she's a nut case.

"How would you like to go to South Korea?" she asks excitedly.

"Would I like to go to South Carolina?"

"No, South Korea. You know, South Korea near China."

"Anita, are you on drugs? What is your problem? It is too late at night for jokes!"

"Phyllis, I am serious. How would you like to go?"

"I don't know, 'Nita. Why would I want to go?"

"To shop, of course. Do you know you can get knock-offs of Gucci, Louis Vuitton, Chanel and all of the top name designers? ('Nita loves to shop; I love to travel.)."

"Nita, it is almost twelve o'clock. If you can find a way to go to South Korea for less than $800, including accommodations, I will go. Now, can I go back to sleep?" (I know she can't do it.).

"Ok, Ok. I'll call you tomorrow, but don't forget your promise." She emphasizes promise.

"Can I go back to sleep now?"

"All right, sleepy head. I'll call you tomorrow. Goodbye."

I don't even tell her goodnight. I just hang up, hoping she comes to her senses and forgets the whole thing. Maybe she didn't call. It must have been a bad dream. I drift off to sleep thinking about what a shop-o-holic 'Nita is. She would go around the world for a sale.

When I awoke I was sure that I had dreamed it all, so I forgot it. A few days later, the phone rang. It was 10:30 PM. It was 'Nita. She was excited and said she had found out all the information and could book the trip. She said, "If you apply now you can have a passport in six weeks." It hadn't been a dream. She was serious. She kept reminding me that I promised I would go.

In April 1988, I found myself at the airport with 'Nita, ticket and passport in hand, on my way to Seoul, South Korea for eight days. We had packed lightly in anticipation of doing lots of shopping. The flight plan was to leave Indianapolis, fly to Pittsburgh, and take a commuter to New York. I was tired before we got started. We were joined in New York by a few friends who are like 'Nita – chronic shop-o-holics.

We waited at Kennedy Airport for Korean Airlines, and boarded the jumbo jet. I couldn't believe I was going across the world. We had breakfast, lunch, dinner, and a snack; watched a movie, and tried to sleep on the plane. The only stop had been Fairbanks, Alaska, for forty-five minutes. The following morning, we were awakened by flight attendants with warm towels to wipe our faces, and toothbrushes. It had been about twenty-three hours since we left home, and I was stiff from sitting.

Two hours later, we arrived in Seoul, South Korea. I was exhausted and couldn't wait to get to the hotel. Our hotel, the Sheraton-Walker, was beautiful, and our room was well appointed. There were beautiful terry robes and house slippers for us.

'Nita couldn't wait to take a cab downtown. For me, it was quite a culture shock. I had been to Europe and found it different, but this was really strange to me. I had trouble wrapping my tired mind around the sights and sounds of South Korea. The streets were crowded with vendors and hundreds of shops. Gucci purses and suitcases were priced so low I almost hyperventilated. It was too much. I was disoriented and jet lagged, and to 'Nita's disgust, I had to return to the hotel early. The following day, 'Nita joined some friends and shopped till evening. I had to stay in bed. And…I wasn't able to get out of bed the next day. Then, for five days, we shopped non-stop, buying purses, suitcases, watches and clothes.

After days of shopping, I finally convinced 'Nita that we needed to take a tour of the city. We boarded a bus to see Seoul, Korea. Several American veterans and nurses who had been stationed in Korea years ago, were on the tour. They had come for a reunion.

Korea has beautiful mountains. There is as much traffic as any large city. Some of the buildings have unusual shapes. The last stop on the tour was the DMZ (demilitarized zone). This is the military base that divides South Korea from North Korea. At the base, we were shown a film about the Korean War. It was heart rending to see families separated and to listen to veterans talk about war atrocities. I looked up and saw what appeared to be bird cages atop a pole, about 14-feet high. I asked why they were there and if birds were in them. The tour guide said there were birds in the cages, and the purpose was to alert them. If the North Koreans sent poison gas through the air, the birds would die first, allowing the military time to make a speedy departure.

We were asked if we wanted to go across a bridge to an observation tower where we could look over into North Korea. Of course, we wanted to go. As we stepped on the bus that would take us across the bridge to the tower, we were told: In the unlikely event that war should break out, the first action taken would be to blow up the bridge. If that happened, we could be on the bridge, or on the other side of the bridge, close to North Korea. Needless to say, this gave me pause. 'Nita paid no attention and just hopped on the bus. I think all the shopping had affected her brain. I felt that I had held my breath till we left the tower and returned to safe ground. I breathed a great sigh of relief and looked forward to the box lunch, which was part of the tour package.

We took our boxes and sodas and sat on the grass near the bus. In the background, we could hear gun shots coming from North Korea. Nobody knew at what they were shooting. I opened my box, and to my delight, there was Kentucky Fried Chicken! What a treat to be so far away from home and have KFC that tasted just like it does at home! I was a bit homesick.

We went back to the hotel and rested for the remainder of the evening. The next day, 'Nita tried to shame me into more shopping but it didn't work. She shopped, and I slept.

The day finally arrived to return home. I didn't look forward to the grueling trip. Would I do it again? I don't think so. It was a great adventure, but I don't think I'll ever answer the phone after 11:30 PM again.

Sometimes I'm not sure: Did I really go to Seoul, South Korea, or was it a dream?

What If

W
hat if I had been born in the 1800s? Would my life have been awful?

What if I have been born wealthy? Would my life have been easy?

What if I had been named June or Janet? Would I feel the same when my name was called?

What if I was fluent in many languages? Would it make me feel superior?

What if you could speak a name and change your future and erase the mistakes of the past? Would you do it, if you could?

What if every opportunity was an entrance to all good and perfect things? Would you seize that opportunity? What do you think would happen if you did?

What if you would just live, giving, and loving life? Would opportunities find you? I think they would. Happenstance, serendipity are just words.

Opportunities come and go. Some are good for you, others aren't. We can only hope we make the right decisions.

Lamenting over the lost opportunities is just a waste of the time that you have left.

That's what I think.

What do you think? After all, it's your opportunity.

Time

There are three things that I feel that are my greatest accomplishments. The first was the birth of my daughter.

The second was a "hysterectomy," which came when my daughter was in her thirties. It freed me from monthly pains and buying those feminine products. Sometimes, it was embarrassing when you went to a store and had to ask where the products were located. The clerk was always loud when she pointed out the location. Freedom from that is a great accomplishment.

The third was a trip to Europe. Going to London and seeing Big Ben; to France seeing the Champs Elysees and the palaces; Italy, with its fountains and beautiful churches. I regret that my mind is fuzzy now. I can't seem to even spell the places any more.

When I went to Europe, I was a wide-eyed tourist who wept practically everywhere I went. The Eiffel Tower was much larger than I imagined. I wept as I walked down the Champs Elysees. The Sistine Chapel, with its beautiful ceilings and statues brought me to my knees. Its beauty was overwhelming. We barely had time to take in what we had seen before it was time to move on.

The tour guide made us feel as though we were there at the Coliseum and the Circus Maximus. I was waiting for the chariots. When I was in Hyde Park, arguing with an African man who stood on a box was especially memorable. He had asked me about my nationality and why I felt I was an American. This is something I will never forget. I think he might have been sorry he asked! I didn't know how proud I was to be American.

With all that I saw in London, Paris, Rome, and Spain, nothing touched my heart like an elderly woman in Geneva, Switzerland. Geneva was such a quiet, beautiful place with clocks everywhere. In the park, they had a clock as large as a fourth of a block, but round of course, made of flowers. It was a working clock.

Everyone seemed polite and would go out of their way to give directions. One afternoon, I took a walk along the water near the park. I sat for a while and noticed a well-dressed elderly lady. She was sitting and staring at the water. I got up from my bench to walk a bit further. I passed this lovely, distinguished lady. As I passed, she said, "Madame, would you wind my watch."

I was taken aback by her request. I sat down and she held out her small delicate, vein-covered hand. Her diamond rings glistened in the sunlight and her watch was rose-colored with diamonds and rubies. "I am afraid to wind your watch ma'am. It is so beautiful; I'm afraid I might break it," I said.

"Don't be afraid, my dear, it is only a watch. It's just time," she said.

Home

I have traveled to many locations looking for that special place. I thought that when I went to Rome and saw the fountains and churches and heard the voices of people speaking in Italian that would be the city where I would want to stay forever. I loved the city, but it didn't fill that hollow place in my soul. The place I could call home. I tried to find a place of peace and excitement in Paris lights, London's Big Ben, and Spain's bullfighting.

I knew here in the USA, that I would find it in South Carolina or surely Georgia where my mother, grandmother, great-grandmother, and great-great-grandmother lived. They loved their home and the soil it was built on. Red dirt had a special meaning for them. There is no magic for me! Funny, I don't keep Georgia on my mind.

Where is the place for me? It took many years, but I found it. There is a book titled "It's All In Your Mind". Maybe I could have found my Shangri-La before if I had had the mind to do so. I don't know if it has happened because I have aged and mellowed, but it has happened.

The place where I can think, relax, enjoy nature, and have a drink of my choice is right outside the family room door to the screened-in porch. It is my haven where I can be alone and yet enjoy birds calling out to each other, squirrels chasing each other, and the sound of cars passing and the sound of wind chimes. I can completely lose myself sitting, listening, and meditating and praying. Many of my problems are solved while sitting on the screened-in porch; and many problems cease to be problems. This is the place I call home. I don't care to ask for more.

Red Hat And Wrinkles

I t was a beautiful day. The tree in my front yard was resplendent with leaves of brown, yellow, and a few green ones that refused to give up knowing the others would blow away and winter would soon follow. I could see the bird's nest so meticulously woven together. I wonder if the birds will remember where they left them in the spring.

I was on my way to the office early. I wanted to go to the cafeteria and have breakfast. I could hardly wait. Having someone prepare breakfast for me would be a real treat.

The drive to the office seemed shorter than usual. There was smooth music on the radio and the weather was perfect. It was about 60 degrees or so. I could lower the car windows and enjoy the breeze.

I had to park quite a distance from the building. I didn't mind and I walked slowly to drink in a bit more of the incredible weather. I knew it was going to be a fantastic day!

When I reached the cafeteria, the smell of coffee hit me. Hmm! I ordered a big breakfast. Oh, wow! The vice-president of the company sat down just as I was preparing to leave. He always had a way of making you feel at ease, and I always enjoyed our chats. I lingered far too long because I enjoyed the company.

I excused myself and picked up my tray to leave. Then, he asked with a smile, "Phyllis, do you have something growing out of your head?" Balancing the tray with one hand, I reached up and realized I had left a big ol' pink roller right on the top of my head. What an embarrassing moment. I thanked him and hurried off. I should wear a hat every day; and I thought this was going to be a great day. Oh well, it had to get better.

A few weeks later, I was sitting at the same table I had sat at before. This time I was sitting alone. Thank goodness! I finished my breakfast and started to get up. I looked down and to my amazement I saw the foot to my pantyhose – not the ones I was wearing – but the ones I had pulled off with my pants a few weeks ago. I had carefully hung up my pants and, unknowingly, had hung up my pants with the pantyhose still inside. OH, NO! I reached down and tried to push the pantyhose up my pant leg with my other foot before I was noticed. Not a small feat, I can assure you. No luck. I got up very gingerly, placed my tray on the conveyer belt, and took tiny steps to the restroom. I pulled the darn pantyhose through my pant leg and put them in my purse. I needed a rest; my days were not going well.

That was it; there were a few things I absolutely must do. First, get lots of rest. Then go full-length mirror shopping so I can check myself from head to toe before I leave the house. The bathroom mirrors don't show me the whole picture. There are times when living alone can be down-right inconvenient. No more fashion faux pas!

Later that afternoon I went mirror shopping. I found the perfect one and carefully mounted it in the hallway. I was so proud and invigorated. I decided to clean out my closets and donate to the Condo Community Annual Rummage Sale. I had been too tired in the past – I had only missed about ten. I was starting to feel a bit guilty. So, I pulled out dishes, sweaters, silly hats and, of course, those pants that held onto my pantyhose.

The following day I got up early, boxed my donations and took them to the clubhouse. It was delightful to greet and chat with my neighbors. The sale tables were stacked high with clothing and household items.

Later that afternoon, I returned to the clubhouse to see if any of my "old treasures" had sold. I was thrilled everything had sold, including those darn pants.

Then I turned to go and there it was at the end of the table. For a moment everything seemed to be in slow motion. It was a red velvet vision of loveliness. I could see nothing except that hat. It could have been worn by Greta Garbo, Joan Crawford, or Betty Davis in a movie in the thirties or early fifties. I am awestruck and in love with "THAT HAT." It is bright red with a wide black ribbon around it. The small brim is turned up on one side. IT IS GORGEOUS and looks very expensive! Surely it has never been worn.

I had inherited the hat gene from my mother. She loved hats and had boxes of them of all descriptions. In her day, hats and gloves were a must to wear everywhere.

A neighbor interrupted my thoughts by saying, "Why don't you take that hat? You seem to be admiring it." I thanked her profusely and left hurriedly before she changed her mind. Who would give up such a stunning hat? I couldn't wait to get home to try that beauty on. I had a suit and shoes that would compliment that hat.

Now that I have a full-length mirror, there will be no more "pink curler capers" or "pantyhose mishaps." I will check myself out from head to toe before I leave the house.

It was early evening when I arrived home. My plan was to take a shower. So, I took off all my clothes and headed for the shower and maybe curling up with a nice book. But wait, I must try on that hat. When I wear it, I will be dressed in sartorial splendor. The choir at church will elbow each other and ask, "Where did she get that beautiful hat?"

I put on my favorite black suit and red shoes with the 3-inch heels that I should have given away. As I stood in front of the mirror admiring my well put together outfit, the phone rang. I turned from the mirror and went into the den to answer the phone. Before I realized it, my friend and I had talked for over an hour. Of course, the main topic of conversation was that hat. As we talked, I cradled the phone between my head and shoulder and removed all of my clothes. It had gotten dark outside so I switched on the light. I got up and went to the hallway. I had forgotten about my new mirror. There I stood to my surprise – as my mother would say – "NAKED AS A JAYBIRD IN WHISTLING TIME" with nothing on except the hat and red shoes with 3-inch heels. Needless to say, I was a sight to behold. I can assure you. I laughed till I cried, then laughed some more. I said, "Girl, you need some ironing!" A red hat and wrinkles; what a combination. Now when I see a lady in a red hat it makes me smile, sometimes even giggle.

I can't do anything about my wrinkles but no more red hats! Well, maybe.

Morning Ritual

E very morning, I wake before the alarm. This time is used to give thanks for waking and trying to recall a dream, if I had one, and to try to make some sense of it. I have not moved or given any indication that I am awake. If so, my husband will attempt to engage me in conversation. Trying to step out of bed without waking him takes quiet moves. If I am successful, I tip-toe to a room where I have books and comfortable furniture. I pick up my books with a meditation for the day, sometimes followed by reading scriptures. My favorite scriptures to begin the day are usually from Psalms. I often read longer than I intend to.

I am reading a book now about addictions that most of us have. It's extremely interesting. I found avoidance is my addiction. I'm working on it!

Oh, no! I hear my husband stirring. As soon as he wakes up, the television goes on. No matter what time he wakes up, there is always a basketball game on, and he wants to discuss it. He just doesn't get that I still have my morning deep voice. I haven't finished what I was reading. I haven't had my coffee! By now he should know the drill. Quiet time in bed, (no touchy, feely stuff), please! Prayer, meditation, and coffee.

How can anybody function without coffee? I get it; he doesn't drink coffee! I must convince him how wonderful the day would be if you start it with coffee.

God bless the one who discovered the coffee bean!

Enough Is Enough

F orty years ago, I gave little thought to the parts of my body. Every part was working perfectly. Now every part needs regular maintenance. Why? I tried to keep all my parts well oiled and hydrated. I would occasionally eat vegetables. No Brussels sprouts, please. Now almost every day there is an appointment to maintain some body part: Physical therapy for my ankle, check-ups for my thinning bones, every three months to check my cholesterol and triglycerides, and whatever else they can find in my blood. My back hurts occasionally and my daughter, grandchildren, and my ex-husband sometimes give me a dynamo of a headache.

Lord, it seems to me this is quite enough. I'm really not complaining. I accept that my parts don't work the way they used to, but please can you tell me why I have cellulite. I understand that even movies stars are admitting to having it, but that doesn't make me feel any better. Enough is enough!

I Won't Be Silent

I come from a family that usually kept secrets. No one wanted to tell the old stories about slaves and masters. Most tried to say they were fortunate enough to have had a humane slave master. For the most part, that was a lie. No one questioned where my grandfather got his blue eyes, 'til I came along. I had a need to know. So, I researched to find the family that my grandfather was attached to. I found the family. No one in my family seemed interested in the information. I felt then and now it matters. I haven't kept silent about it. I felt a freedom, a release, a way to forgive and move on.

It's always easier to dismiss the things that wound our spirit and look for the good. Wounds are deep and slow to heal. Hiding and dismissing seems to be a way of life. One of the bigger problems hiding in plain sight is the HIV/AIDS pandemic. Thousands of men, women, and children die every minute. Children starve and die every day. They are abused and forgotten. It steals our joy and sometimes our lives. Not speaking of it doesn't make it go away. I will not join in with the hordes that pretend not to notice when there is prejudice, death, and injustice.

No one can handle all the injustices of the world, but I can choose not to be silent, and I won't! I have marched. I have spoken, discussed, and ranted. I have been racially disrespected. I will not be silent about the things that really matter!

Speak your mind even if you have to whisper.

The Will To Step Out

I had waited so long just to see him. He had changed my life in so many ways.

Lost after divorce, trying to find myself; searching everywhere to find answers. There was no hope, there was no joy, and there was no love. I was bereft; a diminutive boat on an enormous ocean, being shifted from side to side, trying to hold on. I tried in every way I could think of to find myself again. What about my faith? I thought it just wasn't working for me. God was silent. Perhaps He didn't care or had other things to do.

Needing to step out and communicate with people that I thought would understand, I joined another church. Everyone there was friendly and welcoming. I was invited to join a group who wrote letters to prisoners who had been incarcerated unjustly for political crimes. I wrote to a prisoner. Though he was well known to a few people, I hadn't heard of him, but I was intrigued by his story. I felt strongly about his stand against apartheid and I prayed for him daily. Prayed! That was a surprise and something I hadn't done for a long time. I prayed for this person for twelve years and as I did so, I started to pray for my own downtrodden spirit and mental release.

After 26 years, the prisoner was released. His name was <u>Nelson Mandela</u>! When he walked out of the prison, lean, handsome, with his head held high and his fist in the air, I felt I had been released as well. I felt free once again. I wanted to shout, to sing, and to dance. Freedom at last! Nelson Mandela helped to unlock a door of my soul that had been closed shut for a very long time.

I know that God uses ordinary and unordinary people. I thank Him for his omnipotence, omniscience and omnipresence. I thank Him for all the children of the world and I thank Him for my life and for yours.

"The greatest glory in living lies not in falling but in rising every time we fall." – Nelson Mandela

Chance Meeting

I walked alone to the IRT (Indiana Repertory Theater) in downtown Indianapolis. Parking was at a premium. Men stood in the shadows and made remarks just beneath my hearing. I was frightened, but I kept my head up and tried to follow the instructions I had been given when I went to New York alone on business. My New York friend told me, "Keep your head up. Look like you know where you are going, and get an 'attitude.'" So…I was trying to work on my attitude. I guess I did it. I got to the IRT, which was several blocks from the parking lot, unscathed.

I was meeting a friend who was always late. Tonight was a fundraiser for some organization, and I felt obliged to go. The Delany Sisters' lives were being staged. I had enjoyed reading the books about the two elderly sisters who lived together. One a dentist and the other a nurse. They had lived fascinating lives. This was during the Harlem Renaissance, a time when talented African Americans lived and worked in Harlem.

Hors d'oeuvres were being served so I sat at a table with a smiling lady who invited me to sit with her. I told her my friend was always late and thanked her for inviting me to sit. Her name is Lois, and we spent an hour just talking about the Delaney sisters, how much we enjoyed their books, and how we looked forward to the evening. After the cocktail hour Lois asked, "May I sit with you?"

"Of course," I replied gratefully. I was so happy for the company. After the show started, my friend arrived, late as usual and out of breath.

It has been years and Lois and I still share books and the theater. She is a dear friend. Ours was an unexpected chance meeting. Or, was she intended to be part of my life? My other friend is still a friend, still always late, and since we are both older, we are both hurried and often out of breath.

Having these friends as a part of my life experience often takes my breath away. I am so grateful for all the "chance" meetings in my life, especially the chance meeting with Lois.

Signs

When I was young, older people always said, "When the weather is damp, I can feel it in my bones." Now that I am older, I believe it is true. I have researched the "old wives tales" and according to Google, the weather cannot affect your bones. I choose to believe the old wives because I am now one of them, and I know it's true!

Fortunately, or unfortunately, truth is not the same for everyone. Ask a politician. Many cannot be moved by what is really true. People tend to invent what they believe as true to them and their circumstances.

Thus, signs and omens. I can't remember too many, but I must smile when I remember my mother saying, "If you can shake salt on a bird's tail you can catch him." I never tried it. I thought it would be wasting salt, and I didn't want to catch a bird, anyway. Then, there was, "Step on a crack, break your mother's back." I find myself sometimes avoiding cracks.

Some petunias came up in a pot in the front yard voluntarily. I guess no one told them petunias were to be planted every year. I know it's a sign, but a sign of what? I have no idea. I don't carry a rabbit's foot; have a lucky number or omens. Perhaps, I should. Well, I think not.

I do believe in prayer! That's the greatest sign and wonder of all.

Back When I Was

There was a time when I was full of energy. I would jump out of bed. I couldn't wait to see what the day would bring. I would say to myself, "Bring it on, I'm ready!" There was no problem or project I thought I couldn't handle. That was way back when I was younger.

Now I lie in bed and contemplate what this day will bring and hope it won't go by as quickly as the previous one. I hope and pray today will be full of joy and I will receive no bad news. Like Evaline in The Wiz: "Don't bring me no bad news."

Back when I was 20, 30, 40, 50, and 60, I loved a challenge. Now, I just want to rest, look out the patio window at the trees, birds, rabbits, and the golden retriever next door who is getting older, too. I bet she can remember, too.

Miracles

I marvel at the changes of the season. It's miraculous that in the fall the trees shed their leaves. Most birds head for warmer places. Squirrels build their nests in trees. Animals make preparation for cold weather. Sometimes, we procrastinate and wait 'til winter.

The birth of a baby is miraculous.

It is miraculous how we find stories tucked away in our memories. Our wondering ushers in those thoughts that have hidden themselves or lain dormant 'til the right time to come out. Each new story is released and brings to the light something that has been lying dormant in our minds and hearts. What a miracle the mind, heart, and body are! We are wonderfully made and God has given us different life experiences. That is truly miraculous.

It was truly miraculous that all of the miners in Chile were brought to safety after 69 days underground. The ingenuity of man is truly amazing. The miraculous happens every day. The fact that I am here is miraculous! I am grateful!

Blue Eyes, Elephants, And Moths

When I was eight years old, there was a family who lived behind us. The couple had two children. The children were dark-skinned, had Mediterranean blue eyes and could neither hear nor speak. They never left the back yard to play. Each day I would see them in the back yard. I would walk over and speak to them in some eight-year-old language they seemed to understand. Though they wouldn't speak, I talked to them about elephants and circuses, flowers, trees, and the things my mother told me about joy and laughter. I wanted them to understand whatever sound felt like. We talked endlessly about so many things.

I believe they understood. Often, I asked myself, and them, funny things like, "How do elephants remember?" We agreed moths and elephants must be pretty smart. They have good memories.

My heart longs to see the blue-eyed children again. "Would he be bald? Would she have gray hair? Would they remember? Do they still live? Where are they now?" We would talk again about life, love, and about elephants and moths.

Just one more talk with the blue-eyed children. Eyes, whether brown, green, gray, blue, or purple: Whatever the hue, let's hear it for the eyes!

It's All A Game

I t isn't fair. I've reached the point where I have less time to do all the things planned.

When I was twelve, it took forever to become sixteen. After sixteen, will eighteen never come? And the time waiting to become twenty-one seemed like a lifetime. I thought the world would change at twenty-one and I would be the one to do it.

Who knows, I might be the one to find the cure for cancer, or think of something no one had ever thought of before. Fat chance, Huh!

But, life whizzed by and I find myself doing a countdown. How much time is there and is there something I've left undone?

My Aunt Minta, who is in her eighties, has a Bucket List (you know) things she wants to do before she kicks the bucket. First on her list was a balloon ride; and she did. I'm so proud of her.

I just don't want to make a list. There is too much finality in that. I have already outlived many of my friends. So, I guess I have been left here for something. What?

I have reached the age where I attend at least two funerals a month. Life is like a game. In the end, we win or lose depending on our faith and perspective.

It is my intention to win!

Winning means I will do whatever I have been assigned by God to do. There is so much I can say on this subject, but I won't. I'm getting a little depressed.

Maybe I'd better start that Bucket List.

I should be working on my memory. What am I supposed to be doing? I can't remember.

Travel, Maybe

T here was a time when the thought of travel filled me with so much joy. Packing clothes and deciding what outfit would be appropriate for which occasion made me almost giddy.

I became a child again. I could hardly wait. I was looking forward to hearing my favorite songs sung in a foreign language again. It made my heart leap with joy at the thought of it. Europe, Rome, and Paris. To walk down the Champs Elysees and see the Eifel Tower. Perhaps, I can go to some cabaret and hear someone sing old Edith Piaf songs. I love La Vie En Rose and anything sung in French.

Maybe I could go to Switzerland and see the clock made of flowers. That was a fantastic sight. Or, maybe I'll just clean out the closet, put new hangers in and simplify things. I'll place my suitcases in plastic and put them in the garage awaiting another dream.

I'll just get some Frank Sinatra and Edith Piaf music, and just listen and sit down and enjoy!

Packing and preparing is just too much for my aged body. It is no longer an adventure. Dreaming is so much easier. Maybe I'll make the effort next year.

I can sit in the Lazy Boy I just ordered, turn on the Travel station on TV and just kick back.

Ah…that sounds much better. This thought makes me euphoric. Getting rid of clutter and noise is just delicious. Is this what getting old feels like? If so, I think I like it!

Behind The Door

My father was a gregarious man. Everyone seemed to love him. Often on summer nights, men from all over the neighborhood would congregate on our front porch. Sometimes, they stayed so long, especially on Saturday, that dad would ask them to go home. I can hear him say, "Why don't you go home if you have a home to go to?" Everyone would laugh and no one was ever offended. But they still stayed a while longer. The men talked about sports, mostly baseball, and boxing. Dad was a great host. Sometimes, I listened behind the door to hear what they were talking about. Tonight, they were talking about a young man who came over often. He was a bit younger than the other men. I think he may have been around twenty-four. He was a very nice, polite young man who was married and had young children. I really liked him. Tonight, I was eavesdropping, and I heard one of the men say, "Did you hear about Robert?"

"What about him?" dad asked. "He didn't come over for our Saturday discussion."

Slim, who lived a few blocks away, said, "Don't you guys read the papers? The paper said in bold letters Robert Watts is held for murder. I screamed and almost gave away my hiding place behind the door. I couldn't believe it. Slim went on with what he read in the paper. I was frozen with fear. He described in gross detail how a woman was killed and said Robert was being held for the murder. Even at twelve years old, it sounded like a setup. But what did I know?

When the newspapers came, I read every one. My parents tried to hide the newspapers, but I found them and I listened to the radio. It was on every day and night. Robert would be tried and executed for murder. Robert pleaded that he was innocent. After two years and evidence that was not conclusive, the time came for Robert to be executed. He proclaimed his innocence to the end. I can still see his eyes after all these years. I believed he was innocent and I always will. His eyes haunt me still. It's been over sixty years. I think his name should be said today.

Mother's Board

I know why old ladies wear funny hats! During the long and evil days when black people were enslaved, they had nothing except themselves and each other. And, of course, their faith. Sundays were a day of rest sometimes. Often, they had to slip away into the woods, turn a tub upside down to muffle the sound of their singing. They sang songs like "Swing Low Sweet Chariot" coming for to carry me home and "Golden Slippers" I'm given to even outshine the sun.

Years later – when they were free to go to church – for them it was a privilege and hats and gloves were a must. Often, hats got passed down to the next generation. Hats were like crowns, a sign of a life well lived!

In the old Baptist church that I attended when I was a kid, I met Mrs. Bingham. She was short, plump, and smelled of Tabu cologne and talcum powder. I loved her, and she always pulled me close to her huge, soft bosom and gave me a hug that almost smothered me. I never saw her without a hat, even in the house.

She always sat on the front row of the church along with the other hat-wearing, plump ladies. I think their job was to keep young ladies in line and to make a steady rhythm with their feet. They knew how to sing those old songs like "I Love the Lord he heard my cry and pitied every groan." They could sing it for thirty minutes. I remember one Sunday she whispered to me very sweetly, "Dear, your skirt is too short." I didn't mind. I didn't wear that skirt again.

She often invited me to her home, which was neat, but there was so much furniture. She always baked wonderful pies and cakes and that was one of the reasons I loved to go to her home. I miss Mrs. Bingham, her hugs, and her hats. It brought tears to my eyes to think of her today. I long for the days when ladies wore funny hats and sat on the front row at the church. They represented love for God and a love for everyone. Those ladies on the front row were called the "Mothers' Board." Young people could use a Mothers' Board with quiet dignity and respect. I really think they would love it as much as I did.

Just A Little Worry

I have spent far too much time worrying! It has dominated my thinking for years.

My mother was a worrier. Some things we both worried about did come to pass. Perhaps fifty percent chance it did so…there is a big window of chance that the negative thing I spent so much time thinking about won't happen at all.

My daughter has also inherited the "worry gene" and she doesn't mind sharing her worry, not realizing I have worries enough for both of us.

It's like an itch I can't scratch; it's always there lurking. That dark little thing hovering over me like a cloud. I resolve henceforth to scratch that worry itch!

In my meditation time, I am going to ask for that peace that passes all understanding. I wonder how that would feel. Now, I'm worried it won't happen. There is so much to worry about. I could make a list, but it would be too long and I would worry that I left something out.

Oh, woe is me, when it comes to worry I'm a wretch undone. I promise, God, this is it. It says in your word in Jeremiah, You know the plans You have for me to prosper me and not harm me. So…I guess I should relax and let You take care of all the things I worry about. But, what if You have other things to do and can't get around to it? "I tell You, God, I'll just worry a little bit 'til You have time to take all my worries. Is that a deal? Oh thank You Lord." Just one more thing, could You hurry!

I've heard it said if you worry, don't pray. If you pray, don't worry. OK, OK, I'm working on it. But don't rush me! You know better than anyone, patience is <u>not</u> one of my strong suits. After all, I do believe a little worry strengthens your character.

That's The Way It Is

T aking care of my own responsibilities was as much as I could handle. I paid little attention to the news. I only listened for the end to hear Walter Cronkite say, "And that's the way it is." I did start to listen when young John Kennedy became president of the United States. I loved him. His voice, demeanor, eloquent manner, beautiful wife and children brought a freshness and nobility to dull politics as usual. He won the election in spite of the hate mongers who didn't want a young man or another Kennedy, or a Catholic in as president.

I think when John Kennedy gave a speech, I could hear a kind of pride when Walter Cronkite said, "And that's the way it is." Later, I listened in disbelief when Walter Cronkite said, "The president is dead!" I sat dumbfounded watching Walter Cronkite remove his horn-rimmed glasses as tears dropped from his eyes and said, "That's the way it is," with pain in his voice. I cried too!

We now have a new president; young, eloquent, brilliant, full of hope, with a beautiful family, who is hated for everything past and present. I pray the day will never come when a television announcer will sadly announce our president is dead! And...I might say and "That's the way it is!" It never ends. It's so hard to kill hate. It just won't die!

And...That's the way it is!

Pets In Heaven

My friend, Mary Beth and her family had a beautiful golden retriever. He had been trained to go with her to nursing homes. The residents of the nursing homes were overjoyed to have this beautiful, gentle, loving, well-trained dog to cuddle with and stroke. The dog loved it, too.

One day, the children were playing in the yard with the dog and one was eating an apple. One of the children across the street threw an apple into the street and the dog ran to retrieve it. A lady was driving too fast and hit the dog. She was drunk! "I don't have time to stop," she slurred. The children were heartbroken as they held the dying dog down in their arms. The dog passed away and there were no apologies from the drunken lady who turned out to be a principle of a school. The resident of the nursing home grieved along with the family. "She ought to go to jail," one elderly lady wailed. She missed the gentle dog. She called him God's dog.

Six months later, the family got the news that there would soon be a litter of purebred golden retrievers. The family could hardly wait for the adoption to go through. Finally, the puppy was born, and the family drove to Michigan to pick up the puppy. They named him Shane. My friend brought him over and placed him in my lap. What a beauty, just like a newborn or some newborns, he slept. After a year, he weighed about eighty pounds. He has been to school and passed all his classes with a 4.0 grade point average. He came into the nursing home and shared his love of people and being petted. He's God's dog!

I have never been much of a dog lover. My preference was cats because they don't bother you and mind their own business. I doubt people in nursing homes would enjoy cats. Cats can only be petted when "they" want to be.

I've been told there will be no pets in heaven. Why the heck not? Some have led exemplary lives, giving and fetching and loving. I know; I know what the Good Book says. "We are a spirit and those that worship Him must worship Him in 'spirit' and in truth!" I take exception. Of course, I take exception to so many things these days. Why should pets in heaven be any different?

I'm just not having it!

It's All In Your Head

I wish I had a switch to turn off all the noise and conversations, music that goes on in my head. Often it's distracting and I have trouble separating all that goes on. Some things are automatic, like humming a tune as you drive along, wondering if the man holding the "going out of business" sign is really homeless, listening to your cell phone ring, hoping your children are well and wondering what you will have for supper. To add to this two fire trucks pass, and I must pull over and give them the right of way.

One day when I was busy doing all the things I mentioned while in my car, I noticed a long flat-bed truck directly in front of me. Many trees had been uprooted by a tornado just a few blocks from my house. I was thinking about all those beautiful, mature trees gone and the neighborhood devastated. As I continued looking at the flat-bed truck, I heard a voice gently say, "Get over in the left lane now!" Without question, I followed the order. All the trees flew off the back of the truck. If I hadn't changed lanes the trees would have gone through my windshield. I drove about a quarter of a mile and pulled into a service station and cried and shook. The gas station attendant came to my window and asked if I was all right. I said, "I am more than all right. I am blessed!"

When I told my daughter what happened she asked, "What did the voice sound like, Mom?" I couldn't answer her question. I'm just glad I heard it.

Where Are You From?

I am from divorce, far from it. It's been more than thirty years since divorce. Why does it still haunt me? Why does it still matter? Why do I care? It's like the feeling of death of a loved one. There are reminders: a special song you shared, visiting a city you went to with him, a line from a poem. Remembering for a moment only the good things like travel, the ballet, operas, and the gathering of friends who felt we were the perfect couple. What did they know?

Then, like an arrow through my heart and the pain in my head, I am jarred back to reality. I thank God that I moved on, and a man came into my life who loves, supports, and if necessary, would die for me! Happiness, joy, and contentment well up in me like a bubbling stream. I am from divorce, far, far from it and now, I know this time I will never be from it again!

Bananas

I t was still summer; the grass and trees were green and beautiful. The flowers were in full bloom, the purple iris, roses, daisies, and hosta were a delight. As much as I have enjoyed it, I knew winter would follow summer and fall. I heard there would be a bitter winter. Of course, newscasters always said that, "This year we will have a bitter, cold winter." They would say it with authority. They were often wrong. This time, I believe them, so I think why not plan a cruise this winter to get away from it all.

Just as I thought, summer and fall for me seemed to come too quickly. The cruise was set up and we went to the Caribbean. The ship was fabulous with everything on it you would ever want: swimming, the sauna, a different show each night, shops, restaurants, and gambling, if that's what you want. There was food, food, and more delicious food.

I could have stayed on board, but our traveling companions thought we should see one of the islands. I thought, you've seen one, you've seen them all. "Come on," someone said, "you don't want to come this far and not see everything."

"I'm OK," I said grudgingly. Sitting on a deck chair seemed like a better idea to me.

We made preparations to hire a guide. He was waiting for us when we stepped from the ship. I couldn't determine his nationality. He was about 6 foot tall, with olive skin that glowed. His eyes were dark brown; his hair black with streaks of brown. He was so handsome; I'm sure I had my mouth open. When he spoke, I couldn't determine his accent, either. It sounded a bit French, Spanish, and American. His manners were impeccable. He was a nice guy. He suggested we take a drive up the mountain. He stopped after going up the road for several miles. We could see the whole city and the ship from our vantage point.

He showed us a banana tree. I had never seen bananas on a tree before. Some were ripe and ready for picking. I had never given any thought to the growth of bananas. A banana tree seems like a special gift that God gave islanders and us. I thought about that every time my mother made her delicious banana cream pie. Funny how just picking up a banana can stir so many memories.

Sports Weary

What a great time to sit back and drink my coffee! Nothing comes to mind about any sport I have been involved with. I haven't even been a spectator. My husband watches sports almost every waking moment. He can find a basketball game at 3:00 in the morning. Anything with a ball. I get sick of it! Thank God I can watch television in another room.

I was happy that the Butler basketball team went as far as they did. Their coach seems to be a fine man with good work ethic who teaches the young men to work as a team. They seem to have great camaraderie.

I must admit I like the Olympics. My fondest remembrance is the time a runner was coming in last. He was obviously in great pain, but you could see not only the pain in his face, but his determination to finish. It was painful to watch, but everyone waited for the last runner to finish. Then a man jumped over the railing where he was sitting with his family. He ran or walked to the end of the track with the runner. The man who jumped over the railing was the runner's father. He talked, walked, and ran with his son to the end. It was a picture of love. The father felt he had to help his son to the end.

More important than the sport to me is the story behind the sport. What sacrifice did it take to become an athlete? What did you and your parents do to get you there? For every well-known athlete, I'm sure there is a story. That's what I'm interested in. I will leave the watching and participation to them. I am too impatient to spend time watching. I'd rather read. I'm a bit weary to participate. For all those avid sports-minded people, Enjoy! I don't really care!

Up Or Down?

I don't like elevators. Usually they are too slow and that makes me anxious. That's because I tend to be a bit claustrophobic. I have tried to analyze what my fear is. I think it's because I am not in control and I must rely on the company that made the elevator. I fear it will stop between floors and I won't be able to get out. I prefer to have someone on the elevator with me. Anyone will do. I try to make conversation about the weather or anything else that comes to mind. I notice the people who are on the elevator with me, and I can usually describe them. I make up stories in my mind about what their lives are like.

I Spilled My Coffee

We started our trip early. Not with traffic, I thought. I don't like to be on the highway with the big trucks. There are so many these days. Some have little regard for cars or other trucks.

We are on our way to Chicago. It's a short trip. I'm happy about that. It is a warm spring day; the sky is blue with enormous puffy clouds. I often try to go to sleep when I'm riding in a car. I try sleeping because I am terrified riding in a car. I have never been able to understand why. I think I need counseling to work on this fear. It doesn't matter who is driving. I still feel the overwhelming fear. Perhaps it means I want to be in control. I don't know. I need help. My heart starts to race, and I can feel my blood pressure going up. If I see an accident or a crash on the road, I'm a basket case. The worst part, I spilled my coffee.

How Far Away Is My Peace?

I thought as you grow older there would always be peace and serenity. Not so! There is always something or someone to disturb your peace, your thoughts, your meditation, and your prayers. It could be a solicitor on the phone or the door. It could be a friend who has just lost a job, or their business, or a relative, or all of the above.

I believe that they think as you age you have nothing better to do, but listen to their complaints and problems. Sometimes I want to tell everyone with a problem, "Please, I do not walk on water. As a matter of fact, I am not walking well at all." If you haven't heard my tale of woe by now, here it is in part – just a small part. I have a sprained ankle, and I must wear a big ole ugly boot on my left foot. I don't know how I sprained it, but there it is. Everyone knows how I love shoes.

I definitely cannot walk on water in this boot, and I cannot resolve the problems of my friends and family. So…where is the peace I thought I deserved? Where is the serenity? Perhaps, it's on its way. I'll just wait and see. Patience, however, is not one of my virtues. I sure hope it comes soon because I'm worn out. I'm looking every day for that "peace that passes all understanding." Hey, I am, really.

How will peace come: from a child, a pet, a prayer? However it comes, I'll be waiting with tiptoe anticipation. I have my heart and both hands open to receive it. After thinking it over, what would I do without friends who feel comfortable sharing their joys and sorrows with me? I thank God for the confidence they have in me and I in them. I won't have this boot on forever.

When peace like a river, attendeth my way,
When sorrows like sea billows roll;

Whatever my lot, Thou hast taught me to know,
It is well, it is well, with my soul.

Text: Horatio G. Spafford, 1873
Tune (Ville du Havre) Phillip P. Bliss, 1876

Rain

I sat on the sofa looking out my window. I lived in a condo then, in a quiet neighborhood. I loved it there. I turned my master bedroom upstairs into a den. After work, I hurried in, ate a bite, and placed my shoes on the seventh step as I did every day.

Pepper, my beautiful Persian cat, would be sitting on the steps. He had an attitude today because I was late. But, he was happy I had finally arrived. "Hello Pepper. How was your day?" He meowed his usual OK. It is a rainy day, and the rain had slowed traffic. Thank goodness the rainstorm had subsided a bit, and I could sit on the sofa and collect my thoughts.

There is a huge maple tree in my front yard. I could reach out and touch the leaves if I wanted to from my upstairs window. Raindrops still rested on the large, green leaves. I love the rain, the sound of it, and the feel of it on my skin. I am home at last. So…I can look out with Pepper on my lap and enjoy the sound, the pitter patter against the window pane and the birds taking shelter in the branches.

I can rest now. Tomorrow will take care of itself.

The Bowl And The Wooden Spoon

My grandmother had a bowl she used just for mixing her cakes. The bowl had multi-colors of brown, beige, and white. The inside of the bowl had become a bit rough from her years of mixing and scraping and beating. This was Grandmother Sally's favorite bowl for mixing up a cake. When she reached for the bowl and her wooden spoon, grandchildren were in anticipation, waiting to lick the bowl and catch the delicious doughy drippings. I can almost taste it now. It's been years since I actually baked a cake; and the wooden spoon lies dormant in the cutlery drawer unused and hopeful. The mixing bowl is as lonely as the spoon.

My mother was delusional before she passed away. She saw flying ladies and her parents. I wonder if she remembered about Grandmother Sally's delicious cakes, the "big bowl," and the "long-handled wooden spoon."

What Do You Wonder About?

The world is full of wonder! Wonder women, wonder bras, Wonder Bread. "What a wonderful world." Even the word wonderful has been overused and sometimes abused. I wish I didn't wonder so much because wonder is a first cousin to worry. Wonder is very tricky. It can turn to worry when you're not looking. When I am curious about something, Google has saved my day and scratched my itch for learning many times.

All my life, I have had questions; things I wonder about. Will my grandchildren make good life decisions? I wonder about indigo children. I wonder will the child prodigy, Ethan Bortnick, continue to play the piano and conduct as he does now. I wonder when the economy will get better. I wonder about global warming. I wonder if I will ever write anything that is profound and, yes, wonderful! I wonder if there will ever be a cure for cancer. I wonder if my mother, who passed away years ago, ever thinks about me. I just hope she does.

Yes, I wonder about unimportant and important things. I wonder every day, truthfully, every hour. I can say I have never wondered or was curious about what Mona Lisa was thinking about. That's just one thing that has never pushed my curiosity and wonder button.

Curiosity pushes us forward and surrounds us with awe!

Who Am I?

I am the youngest child of two. My brother prayed for a little sister. Here I am. We are both still here. Who knew we would have become what's known as "elderly." I don't feel elderly. Well, I do sometimes. I think he does, too. Times when it's damp outside my bones know it before I check the temperature.

What does it really mean to be elderly and set in your ways? If it means you want your life to have some semblance of order and peace, I guess I am. Whatever I have become, I know Dad would be proud. He was proud of me no matter what I did. He didn't know everything I did. Yes, I was a Daddy's girl! Mother tolerated all my questions with love and grace. I have a bit of trouble with "grace." There are some things that it takes a lot of "grit" to forgive and be loving.

Who am I? The question is a difficult one. I am so many things. I am a person who loves some jazz, some Beethoven, and some Bach, and Bocelli makes me weep and laugh. I could listen to it every day. Why is it that it's done only around Christmas? Every day is Christmas for me! I love to watch dancers, all kinds of dancers, especially ballet. I am a woman full of life with wrinkles and lots of memories. I am satisfied with the life that I have been given. I am blessed beyond measure. I am God's child, still full of wonder and mostly joy. Who I am cannot be confined to paper. I love books. I love to touch them and read as many as I can. I love to look into the eyes of everyone I meet. Sometimes, I can see my reflection in their eyes. I wonder who they think I am. If the eyes are the windows to the soul, perhaps they know.

The Quilt

Y ears ago, and even today, ladies make quilts. In the days of slavery, enslaved women made quilts by keeping scraps of material they found from everywhere. Many quilts were made into directional designs that would point the way to the North. When an escaped slave saw the quilt hanging up, the design in the quilt pointed north, and they knew which way to run and attempt escape.

My mother made a quilt by hand out of scraps of material that she collected over the years. It became an historical quilt. I slept under it often. It made me think of the beautiful work she had done so meticulously. There was a scrap from my brother's and father's shirt. And, a scrap of material from the dress I wore to my first day of school, and scraps from aprons and scraps of clothing from my grandparents' clothes. Mother didn't use a pattern, but all the scraps form perfect circles of unending love.

I loved the quilt and I felt so warm and in touch with my roots. It brought back memories of stories my mother told me about the South. Some good, some bad but mostly good. Not too long ago, I missed my quilt. Where was it? I have checked every place I could imagine. Did someone throw it away not understanding its worth to me? I would pay quite a sum to find it again and hold it close to feel the warmth and comfort it brought.

I cannot accept that it is lost. I think it is just hidden to produce itself just at the right time. Till then, I will hold all of the memories of the quilt in my heart.

Like A Lakota Woman

One morning, an elderly woman sat on the side of her bed. She was full of years and full of pain. She couldn't sleep because of her physical and emotional pain. So…she got up and sat in her favorite overstuffed leather chair. From the chair, she could see through the patio doors to the yard white and glistening with snow. It was a cold day, and she couldn't get warm, even though she covered herself with a knitted shawl. She was in so much pain that she rocked and prayed and rocked and prayed, like a Lakota woman on her mourning stool, but the pain would not leave her. No amount of medicine eased the pain in the mind and body.

Next to her chair, she kept her favorite books. Without looking, she picked up a book about needs. Her need was great, but that wasn't what she wanted to read at this moment. Then she reached for another book entitled "Don't Die in the Winter – Your Spring is Coming." She clutched the book to her breast and repeated the title over and over again. "Don't Die in the Winter–Your Spring is Coming." Your Spring is Coming!

She looked out of the window and saw birds, sparrows, she thought. They were everywhere – hundreds of them. Were they lost? "What can I do," she said. "They surely must be hungry." She got up and looked out the window. To her amazement, a red bird flew by and perched on the fence, then did a beautiful dance of flight over the sparrows. The sparrows seemed to enjoy it. To her right a blue bird flew by and perched on the fence and also danced in flight. The sparrows seemed to enjoy the blue bird's performance, too. A squirrel stopped to take a look in amazement.

What is this about? Can "all" these birds be lost? She wondered for a moment then said, "No, I am lost."

The message is now clear: Don't die emotionally or physically in the winter. My spring is here right now. Immediately, she felt lighter, her pain was gone. She dressed, went outside, thanked God, and fed the birds.

Is It Sunday Again?

The passing of time is different now than it used to be. Days are shorter. At least, it seems that way to me! When I was eleven years old, I couldn't wait to be thirteen. It meant I was finally a teenager! Teenagers have more privileges, or so I thought; but Mom didn't agree. I found I had no more rights than I did at eleven. I was convinced that would really change at sixteen, and it did. So, there were times I wanted to be eleven again, when there wasn't as much peer pressure and decisions to make. Surely at eighteen, I would be able to handle all of life's problems. I knew by then that life was extremely complex, but it would all come together at twenty-one. I would be an adult finally, and I could do exactly as I pleased. How wrong I was. For all the mistakes I made, there were and still are consequences. It seemed that after twenty-one, the days flew by. Before I knew it, I was thirty, and it was past time to really decide who I wanted to be when I grew up. I decided to work hard on my marriage and my career. Only fifty percent of that worked out. My career lasted far longer than my marriage. I should have spent as much time selecting a mate as I did a career. As I said, there are consequences. After thirty years of age, it seemed like two blinks and it was time to retire and devote myself to doing all the things I thought I wanted to do.

At last! Thank God! Maybe time will be kind enough to slow down. If I compare this time of my life to the seasons, this is winter. It is certainly not the winter of my discontent because I am very content. I don't want to return to any other age. This one is just fine. My only concern is that time goes faster at this age than it ever did at any other. It seems almost every other day, I'm saying to myself: "Is it Sunday again?" Not that I'm complaining. I like Sunday, but it comes so quickly.

Tell me, *is it really almost Sunday again?* I can't believe it!

The Bookends

It's housecleaning time again. What can I get rid of to avoid dusting it? How about those old heavy bronze, penny-colored bookends? The Native American on each bookend is in full headdress. Every feather is deeply etched and the faces look distinctive and noble. I wonder if they are a replica of a great chief.

In 1919, my mother and her family moved to Indianapolis from Homer, Georgia. Native Americans inhabited Homer before my mother was born. Mother and her family left their home there because of Ku Klux Klan threats. They came by train, bringing few possessions. Among them were these bookends. I don't know why they brought them because they are so weighty. My grandparents must have considered them precious for some reason. Mother can't remember where they came from originally. They have been around as long as anyone can remember. Perhaps they were made to honor the Cherokee Indians.

I stop dusting to daydream about the Cherokees living in the same woods mother played in as a child. I can remember seeing these bookends on the mantle of my grandparents' home and in my parents' home. My mother gave them to me. They have held three generations of books. Books have always been a part of our lives.

As I dusted the bookends this time, I appreciated their history anew. I can never part with them, except to pass them on to my daughter and tell her why the bookends are so precious and certainly worthy of dusting.

In Search Of Quiggles

Mark Twain once said, "History is a science." Gathering it should be done in a scientific way. Since I am scientifically challenged, that presents a problem. Where and how do I begin my search for Quiggels? What is a Quiggels you might ask? It is not in the dictionary. Quiggels is not a what, he's a who. He was a great man. My mother told me his first name is Ralph. Since he was such a great man, I certainly should be able to find out something about him. Why am I searching for him? Well…I can only answer a few of those questions. I don't know anything about his family. I met him many years ago when I was three years old. As to what makes him a great man, I will let you be the judge of that. I feel without any fear of contradiction I can accept that he was indeed a great man.

I think of him often. I know he retired and moved to Florida. I have searched the census and the directories and have interviewed neighbors who knew him. Their only reply is that he was a very nice insurance man. I would love to find a relative of his to tell them what he meant in my life. The story of Quiggels and Riverside Amusement Park has been on display at the Indiana Museum and told many times by a friend of mine who is a storyteller in churches and schools and has been acted out by actors from Indiana Repertory Theater. I hope that honors my friend Quiggels. I have heard it said, "Some people come into your life for a reason, a season, and some for a lifetime." Quiggels came into my life for a reason, a season, and lifetime. This is why he is a great man to me.

According to Webster's Dictionary, "great" means long continued, notable, and magnificent. To me, he was all of that and more. Every time I see someone nurturing a child, giving sound advice, support, encouragement, or simply setting a good example, I will think of Quiggels. So…the search is over because he is easily found. I know he has never left me. He is right here in my heart.

I Want To Read

I am three years old. It's warm outside. Other children are playing in the street.

I want to read!

Why can't I read?

I am tired of those old books with farms, farm animals and ladies in aprons cooking.

I want to read! There is something in letters I want to read!

Mom helps sometimes, but she said, "You are too young to read."

What am I going to do?

I want to read! Why can't I read?

I stomp my feet and make a face.

Oh, there is the insurance man. He has a funny name. I laugh when I say it.

"Mr. Quiggles, I want to read."

"Then read you shall, Sweet Pea," he replied.

We sat down on the steps of the house and he taught me once a week. I loved to see him. He was always dressed nicely with a dark suit, white shirt and a beautiful tie. He always smelled good, like lavender (that's what mom called it).

Now I can read just like everyone else!

Won't everyone be surprised?

Hooray! I can read!! I am finished with those old Dick and Jane books.

I want more books! No playing in the street for me. Mother isn't quite so pleased. Now she will have to buy more books and she will have to hide her romance magazines. I can't wait to try and read those.

Love's Observation

I have observed my husband for the past eleven years. I've listened to his stories about being in the military for thirty years. His stories are always the same. He takes great pride in the racial barriers he was able to break down. I am proud of him, too. As time goes on, sometimes I must finish a story for him. He is forgetting some of the details. It's understandable; he will be 86 this year. It's hard to believe. He seems to be completely unaware that his 6-foot frame is now a few inches shorter. His memory is not the same, his hair is thinner, and he loses things – almost everything! Sometimes putting his socks on is a project. I'm sure he sees the same things in me. Growing older is a slow process. Thank God! Walking through the mall for over twenty minutes for me is a task not worth the effort. I have immense desire to live a bit longer. I have a few things I would not like to be left undone. Perhaps someone would finish them for me. I doubt it.

I must stay to be with my husband, to love him with all I am, to help with his socks, to find his glasses, and to finish his stories. I can do no less because my love for him goes to the marrow of my bones and to the deep recesses of my soul.

Lord, let our transformation be slow enough that my husband and I will barely see it in each other. Let us love each other just as we are, accepting the faults and foibles. Let love be the eraser of bad times and may joy be the key that will continuously open the door to an everlasting love!

Innocence Lost

I remember a time (before television) when my world was innocent and small. I had little knowledge of world affairs, only current events that affected my life. It was a time when integrity, honesty, friendship, and loyalty were not just words. Those principles were a way of life. Of course, I knew about injustice and prejudice, but it did not manifest itself with such overt hate. It was mostly racial separation.

Since the attack on America, I have felt heart heavy and bone weary. Is this a warning sign to stop the hatred and start to love and appreciate others? I don't know.

I do know, I see life differently now. The sky is bluer, my love is deeper, and gratitude will be a daily part of my life. I will not forget that the Lord is my light and my salvation. Whom shall I fear? The Lord is the strength of my life, of whom shall I be afraid? No One! I agree with the words of David in the book of Psalms. Never will I allow anyone to intimidate or cause me to fear. This is my life and I will live it as long as God allows.

I lack the ability to express my sadness, when I watch the devastation caused by evil people. I have tired of platitudes, posturing, and useless rhetoric, but for now, what else can we do except PRAY! I only have questions, no answers. In the day to come, what can we tell the children? I would like to believe all things work together for good to those who love the Lord and are called according to his purpose. But do I really believe this? I think I do.

Again, another question: What is the purpose of such things? After great introspection, I believe that I know why and I hope you do, too. Is this my innocence and America's lost, or have we ever been innocent? Is this retribution? Have the chickens come home to roost? I pray that this is not the case.

September 13, 2001

Random Thoughts

I have often heard it said, "It I had my life to live over," I'd still do the same things again. There are also those who say, "If I had my life to live over" and know what I know now, I would do things differently. As for me, I'm not so sure. Now that I'm in the autumn of my years in retrospect, I think I would have been more observant, more daring, and even a bit outrageous. Perhaps, I would have flown to the Greek Islands, rented a boat, and sailed around the islands alone, worn crazy red hats, skinny-dipped in the Caribbean, bungee jumped, took sky-diving and ski lessons. Or perhaps, I would have done simple things like sitting in a field of flowers and marveling at the beauty of nature. Maybe, I would speak my mind more or listen to more Bach, Beethoven's Ninth, Blues, and of course the Hallelujah Chorus (even when it wasn't Christmas). I'd dance more, sing more, and eat more chocolate! When you reach the time of maturity, when old friends and acquaintances tell you – you look well – instead of you look great, and doctors and teachers look like they are "eighteen" years old, you know you are getting older.

This is time in my life when I have come to appreciate the things I used to pay little attention to. Things like seeing a rainbow, the shapes of leaves (especially the ginkgo), the color of sunset, the turning of the leaves in the fall, the smell of budding trees in the spring, the brightness of a baby's eyes, and the smooth skin, beautiful designs found in a snowflake, and the understanding of a friend.

What is it about getting older that makes one want to wax philosophical? I wish I could tell all those younger than myself not to waste a single moment wishing you could, and fearing you can't. Dare to dream and dare to fail, then dare to dream and fail again, until you find what you are destined to do, and who you are meant to be. Never be intellectually satisfied and never get angry about things that do not really matter, (at least not for more than three minutes).

I retired from a company where I had worked more than thirty years. Was everything always perfect? Of course not. Did I make a difference? I hope so. I have often had it said to me that I would never work for one company that long. It may not have been a good idea for many, but it seemed to work for me, even though it wasn't my original plan. I never doubted for one moment that God knew exactly what he was doing.

My Brother

When my brother and I were children, we invited a few kids over on Saturday nights. We would sit down and cross our legs at the ankles in front of our enormous RCA radio. The radio was brown mahogany with a lighted dial. The front was a brown woven material that housed the sound. There was some status in having a radio that was about three-feet tall. My parents were very proud of it. I'm sure it was bought at a sacrifice.

Sometimes our friends would sleepover. After the station with ghost stories was over, my brother would start to tell the story about "red eyes and bloody bones" just to send me off screaming to my mother. He loved doing it. Every Saturday night, it was the same thing 'til I was about twelve. Then the stories didn't work anymore. I was growing up and wanted to hear stories with more substance, like "Let's Pretend," on Saturday mornings.

I still have some of that twelve-year-old in me. I like a story that awakens my senses and causes me to pretend about what could have been.

Now, my brother and I are much, much older. The next time I talk to him, I'll ask him if he remembers the big RCA radio, the ghost stories we heard, and what we thought of them. My brother seems to forget some of the stories he told me, but I will never forget that he told them.

I love and cherish my only brother, Jesse, who sat with me on the floor in front of our enormous brown mahogany radio and my parents who worked so hard to buy it.

My Heart Speaks

I am a wife, a daughter, a mother, a grandmother, and a great-grandmother. I have lived a long life. I never thought I would live to see this day. I am undone beyond grief!

Bill is my first grandchild. Did you notice I said "is?" That will never change. I was there when he was born. He was a beautiful child who taught me the art of forgiving and loving. I loved him with all my heart. Unconditionally! He loved the fact that I have written to preserve our family history. He was very proud of that. He came from generations of fine loving and generous people. I have been gifted to a small degree with the language of words. Perhaps, that makes up for not understanding the language of higher mathematics.

Bill was a gracious dreamer who spoke in the language of a dreamer. His spirituality was far beyond my meager understanding. He spoke in a staccato sometimes too rapidly for these old ears to pick up. I knew he loved me, his mother, sister and brother, nephew, nieces, and his friends. And, above all, he loved God. He was kind, sometimes to a fault. I hope that kindness was never taken advantage of. If so, I forgive, because I know he would.

There is so much I would like to say. My use of words has escaped me now. I submit these words: "This is the day the Lord has made. I will rejoice and be glad in it!" We don't get to choose the day; that is the work of a higher power.

Not long ago, I wrote these words. It's called "The River of Life."

You no longer need to stand at the river my dear Bill.
What would you want for us today?

I think you would want us to love God with our whole heart. To be loving, kind, thoughtful. Heads held high against the trivial and the fray. You loved to walk for hours. I walk with you now and forever. I think you would want me now simply to say, "Thank you and go in peace."

Uprooted

I held your newborn body close to my heart. You were warm and snuggled close, too. Without a doubt, you held the key to my heart; a key that would lock us together forever. I thought our time together would be without measure. We were bound together as tight as a ball of twine. How could I know the ball of twine would unwind so soon? The ball is now a string that cannot be wound neatly again. Like a bell that cannot un-ring. And I sit and think and long to hear your voice. The sound of your words. Words that seemed to be musical. Your words seemed to have a staccato rhythm!

Though you are gone, no, no, you are not gone. Just out of sight for awhile! I will forever hold you in my heart. My heart aches and no amount of drugs can deaden this ache. There is no box that can hold your spirit. Feel free to roam as you always did. So, if I must let you go, I release you to the wind, clouds, and the sky, but never from my heart. I will hold you close with every breath. I promise I will never forget!

Will Karen find my books of life? I hope so.

In the book of life, the answers are in the back, so says Charlie Brown.

When I think of the book of life, of course I think of the Bible. I agree somewhat with Charlie. The answers are all through the book. Life unfolds in the beginning when God made the heaven and the earth and a rebellious man and woman, who gave us a legacy of sin and broken relationships, from Genesis to Malachi and from Matthew to Revelation at the back of the book. I guess the question is what do we choose to do with this book of beginnings and endings? I chose to continue to read it daily and reach out to a loving God who forgives and gives me blessings upon blessings, and grace upon grace. In the book,

I find hope, joy, and consolation. The writings of David are especially poignant. I love Psalm 139 where he said we are wonderfully made and God has scheduled our days.

I don't skip to the end of the book too often. I know what the end is.

The Dancer

It's here again: The Indiana State Fair. Many have prepared since last year for these days of heat and hay. I can hear the train whistle from my house. My husband is among the happy ones. He loves to line dance every day. I find excuses not to go. Why am I not excited? This is "The Year of the Pig!" Young people will be decked out in band uniforms hoping to be voted the best. Mothers will push strollers with babies uncovered and unprotected from the brutal sun. I know that the elephants and ponies are exhausted from all the children who must ride on their backs.

As I step from the air-conditioned bus, I am assaulted by the smells, the same ones from previous years. We wait for the shuttle that takes us to the tent, where ladies and a few men will be dancing to the delight of the few watchers. They don't seem to mind that the audience is small. I sit and watch waiting to be bored. I remembered the beautiful dancer from last year. She seemed to dance for her own pleasure, oblivious to everyone else. She dipped and turned. I was mesmerized. She was beautiful with her silver hair; the sun made it sparkle. Then she caught my eye, and it seemed that she started to dance just for me. After the music stopped, she came over and said, "Wouldn't you like to dance?"

Of course, I did for that moment. I wanted to dance. My feet wanted to dance but they seemed useless to me and I couldn't dance. If I could, perhaps I could lose myself in the dancing and forget where I was; but I couldn't. She had turned my attitude around. Her smile changed my day. I no longer noticed the pungent odors and the oppressive heat. I thanked her and hoped that I would see her again.

After the dancing, I saw things differently. People were walking and smiling and having a wonderful time. I no longer cared that the people who sold T-shirts were displaying the same ones from last year. I walked around and watched people eating corn, elephant ears and pork with grease.

So…, I sat down and ate deep-fried green tomatoes and wished I could be a dancer!

A Visit With Miss Pat

My friend, Lois, had asked me on numerous occasions to go with her to meet her 92 year old friend, Pat. This time I acquiesced and told her I would go. We drove to a neighborhood I had passed and knew it was a well-kept neighborhood with beautifully manicured lawns. It was pleasant to see the houses different and unique. As we drove into Miss Pat's driveway, I wondered who took care of her lawn. Lois rang the doorbell and a petite, attractive, well-dressed, white lady answered the door. She was cheery and welcoming.

Miss Pat wanted to go to the "annual block party." She wanted us to see her beautiful collectibles she kept upstairs. Her home was beautifully decorated. The carpets were white. Each room was full of light, not at all what I expected.

Miss Pat had been an architect and she still had pictures of her designs. I was so pleased that she felt comfortable to show them to someone she hadn't met before.

Lois made the arrangements for us to go to the block party. This meant making sure Miss Pat had the right purse, right keys, and the garage opener. Miss Pat wanted to make sure she looked her best. She had just purchased a beautiful print scarf and she was wearing it with what I thought was a white blouse with a starched collar. Tan, belted slacks completed her well put together outfit. She found a purse that still had the tag on it. The purse was an additional complement to her outfit. Before we left the house she had to find her favorite cane. She had several beautiful ones.

We got into the car and drove around the corner to the block party. She assured us that Lois pulling into a neighbor's driveway would be fine. She was right.

Lois had chairs for us in her trunk. As we walked to where her neighbors were having the party, I took Miss Pat's hand and I knew this is a grand lady, beautiful, gracious and full of wisdom. As we neared the group I recognized my cousin and his wife. He had an inquisitive look on his face. The look was like "I can't remember you here and how do you know Miss Pat." We sat down and I explained how I met Miss Pat. My cousin lives across the street and has loved her for all those years.

Miss Pat, I found out, is the darling of the neighborhood. She is loved by everyone and they all look out for her. She walked around and greeted everyone. The neighbors' pets loved her! I fell in love with this lady. I believe her presence gave stability and class to the neighborhood. There is a mixture of races; black, white and Asian, perhaps others that weren't present.

The atmosphere was cordial, pleasant, and there was an abundance of food, good music and face painting for the children.

After about an hour, it was time to take Miss Pat home. Before we left Pat remembered we had met before and she recounted the year, day, place and the occasion. I was embarrassed that I remember little about it, although I am younger than Miss Pat. She also recalled another time that she had seen me and told me what I was wearing. So I wasn't a stranger after all. I was thrilled to know that we had met before, but I regretted the time lost all those years we didn't stay in touch.

Lois told me that she met Pat at church more than 33 years ago. She became a friend to her children and a beloved part of their lives. Lois told me what appeared to be her signature starched blouse is her husband's shirt. He passed away years ago but she continued to wear his shirts. "He was truly the love of her life," Lois said with a grin.

Two hours on a beautiful, cloudless Saturday afternoon in Miss Pat's presence changed my life. I feel richer for the experience. It was like being in the presence of real royalty. I felt she had given love and tranquility to her neighborhood. What could she do to a town or city? I believe positive changes would always take place in her presence.

Thank you, Miss Pat. Who said you can't change "old people?" I am older and you made a difference to me, one I will never forget. I see growing older in a different way now.

You deserve to be remembered so others can be blessed by a life so well lived. You, Miss Pat, face mortality fearlessly and triumphantly. I will try to do the same. You are a force my dear and a precious gift. I can't thank you enough!

Daytime Midnight

I always loved him. He is the strong one, the bright one, the one who is even tempered, handsome, and wise. He has grown older as we all, or most, hope to do. He has lived his life always hoping and dreaming his latter days would always be better than the former ones!

I always wanted so much for him to be happy. Even after over 50 years we love each other. His wife understands the love between a brother and a sister. He has joy and happiness, but he is now legally blind and he only sees in shadows in the daytime and very little at night. When I see him, I can remember all of the many childhood times we spent. They are dreams, like shadows on the backside of my mind. My brother can sense when I'm in the room, even when I don't speak. I think he can remember how we were, all of our lives. His love for his little sister glows through the shadows of his blinded eyes, even though daytime is midnight for him. I know he will remember and smile!

Fat Chance

W hat do I want now?
I want a two-hour massage.
I want my grandchildren to want to know about their heritage.

I want them to succeed in whatever being successful means to them.

I want my husband to find everything he loses around the house.

I want time to sit and meditate.

I want to write poems.

I want war to be ended.

I want to be pain free.

I want to go on one more cruise to the Mediterranean.

I want a three-bedroom condo.

I want a house that will magically clean itself.

I want someone to wake me, dress me and take me to the gym.

I want a puppy that I don't have to walk or clean up after.

I want honest and faithful friends.

I want to live in a way that I will be remembered for some of the funny and ridiculous things I say and do.

I have given up sweets for a month. I want calories removed from all sweets so that you can eat all the chocolate you want and not gain weight.

Right now I just want a chocolate chip cookie!

Promises

Every morning when we wake and even after, a promise is being kept. That promise is God will never leave you or forsake you. What a gift of grace. Countless times family and friends have made promises that they will be there for you and when the going got rough you looked for them and they weren't there.

If we believe God's promise to us, we can forgive those who weren't there over and over and over again. How many promises do we break on a daily basis?

I promise to exercise.

I promise to eat better.

I promise to have a devotion time.

I promise to clean my house.

I promise to visit and call the sick.

How many times do we break our promises?

How many times are we ungrateful? How many times has God been there to cover us with His love even when we were too thoughtless to acknowledge His loving presence? He's been there every time – ready to give and forgive.

Stop, take a deep breath and give the situation to God. He has always taken care of our light afflictions and He always will. What a promise keeper! Just lean back and watch God do it!

Today I promise to do that. Wow, I feel better already!

Fifty-Four

I never thought I would long for the time I was 54. At 54, I was full of energy and new ideas. Going to the gym was a must. My eyes were bright and my hair was full and healthy. I was single and the world was my oyster.

I was so busy with projects that I didn't have time for breakfast. Bacon, eggs and toast might be a once a month occurrence. Coffee and a small cup of orange juice were more my style, or just coffee and a cinnamon roll.

Now over 20 years have passed and my energy and creative level are certainly not what they used to be. Now it's a regimen of medicines to keep me up during the day and pills to help me sleep at night.

At one time I said oh just let it happen, getting old, that is. I'm not going out without a fight. I will get up earlier, exercise more and continue to take all those damn pills. Oh my, but I really do wish I was 54 again! Well, what would I do that I don't do now? Life is good. I can't wait to see what I'm going to do next!

I was in a restaurant while I was contemplating. I then became fascinated by the voice of the young man behind the counter. Where is he from? What is the accent? African? Jamaican? He is the only one wearing a pink shirt. I bet that he doesn't give any thought to being 54. Oh well, life is good.

Rite Of Passage

The whistle blows in the distance now. Train whistles remind me of childhood adventures.

"I dare you to walk across the train tracks," my friends would say. "I dare you!"

It was like a rite of passage. I must walk across the tracks above a trestle. I could see between the tracks to the street below.

Oh how I wanted to be accepted as brave. It took an entire summer to muster up the courage to do it.

Wow, I crossed the tracks to the other side. My friends clapped and shouted. Now I must get back to where my friends were. I had to do it again! And I did it! There was more clapping and shouting.

A few days later my friends admitted they really never had the nerve to cross the tracks. I learned a valuable lesson about wanting the approval of others.

Never Do That Again

What have I done in my life that was wild and crazy? What haven't I done? Too much to list.

Riding sidesaddle on the back of a motorcycle, arms around the waist of a crazy friend is one of them. I couldn't ride astride the seat because I had on a long skirt. I'm sure that this was over 40 years ago. Where did the time go? It seems like yesterday. I can remember the outfit that I wore. It was a favorite. It was made like overalls but of a light-beige denim. I was visiting my friend, Bonita, whose boyfriend, Don, volunteered to take me home.

"I'll be glad to take you home," he said with his infectious, beautiful smile.

"Do you mean on your motorcycle?" I asked.

"Of course; you'll enjoy it. It's only a mile."

"I don't think I can. I'm wearing a skirt."

"Pull it up," he said, grinning.

"I can't do that."

"Well, ride sidesaddle," he said. "Come on, don't be a sissy." I hadn't heard that since I was a kid and I started to remember all of the silly things kids did, and when someone would say, "I double dare you!"

Like a fool forgetting that I was too old to respond to double dares, I placed my fanny on the bike sideways. Big mistake!

He took off before I could change my mind. I knew immediately that I had made a huge error in judgment. I held on as tight as I could around my friend's waist and closed my eyes. I could feel the wind whipping my face. I know I had a death grip on him. I knew I was going to die! I thought, well, Lord, it's my fault not Yours. If I live, I will never do this again.

The minutes that it took to arrive home seemed like an hour. I was so happy to have my feet on the ground. I have never, or at least until now, gotten on a vehicle that has only two wheels again.

I have heard that God takes care of fools and babies. I am grateful for that!

Miss Loraine

T ry as I will, I am unpoetic. If I could write poetry, I would write about Miss Loraine.

    I saw a lady as I went into a supply store to make copies for a project that I was a part of. I was filled with anger, resentment, and regret that I had said yes to be a part of this project. I had a bad attitude and I wasn't having a good day. In addition to that, I hadn't had my coffee. I wondered if the clerks could see there would be no nonsense with me today. Did they see an angry old lady who had grown tired of the vicissitudes of life?

Well, I saw a woman even older than myself. She looked to be in her eighties, her back was bent, dark, coffee-colored skin. Seeing her made me smile and I felt better. My bitterness dissolved as I cheerily said "Good morning." She said good morning and didn't linger for pleasantries.

I made the copies I had come in for and headed for the cashier. A bit of resentment over the task still lingered. Then I saw the lady I had spoken to. She had a cart full of blue folders. Then she placed them on the counter. I heard myself say, "I'll pay for those."

"Those are mine," the white-haired lady said in a gruff voice!

"I know. I'd just like to pay for them."

She cocked her head to the side and asked, "Why?"

"I just want to," I said softly.

"Well, I don't want you to." She kinda flashed a $100 bill. She sounded a bit annoyed, so I said, "OK, if you don't want me to."

"Well, I'll let you do that if you tell me your name."

I said meekly, "My name is Phyllis."

"Your whole name," she practically demanded.

I wrote it down. "And your phone number," she said.

I don't know why I complied, but I did.

She said, "Here is my name and phone number also."

The clerk stood there watching this, not knowing what to do. I wonder what she thought. The clerk said, "There is a poster, too."

I said, "I will pay for that, too."

"Are you sure?" she said.

"Yes, I am," I answered.

"What can I do for you?" the lady asked.

"Just a hug," I replied. In that hug I felt the touch of my mother.

The lady cried and smiled. So did I. My whole day changed when I met Miss Loraine.

My Name Is Doctor Adams
(Working on the Inside)

I sat in another doctor's office waiting for four doctors to privately discuss my case. I was in excruciating pain. A doctor walked into the waiting room, extended his hand and said, "My name is Dr. Adams and I know the cause of your pain." Powerful words, I thought. I had been in pain for five months and this was the tenth doctor I had seen. When Dr. Adams shook my hand I knew he did indeed have the answer. He left the other doctors in conference still trying to figure it out.

A bone scan confirmed that Dr. Adams was correct. "What are my options?" I was almost afraid to ask.

"You can take pain pills and antibiotics until you become immune to them or I can make an incision from the middle of your chin to your ear and scrape your infected jaw bone and remove a tumor that I feel is benign."

"What's the worst that can happen if I have the surgery?"

"Your face may be left with no feeling on one side."

"What about the scar on my face from my chin to my ear?" I was feeling nauseous and light headed.

The incision would be on the inside through your gums to the jawbone. There would be no scar on the outside," he said confidently.

I wrapped my arms around myself as there was no one else to do it. My mind began to race and I thought how God had operated on the inside and it didn't show on the outside except by the way you treat others. There was a time in my life when I claimed to be agnostic. God still loved me even when I didn't love myself. God is Jehovah, Rohi, the God who heals. He is the grand physician and has never lost a case.

Dr. Adams told me about a woman who came to him in such pain she had written a suicide letter and he was the last doctor she decided to see. Maybe she didn't know Romans 8:28. "All things work together for good for those who love the Lord."

I sat for a long time without speaking. Dr. Adams waited patiently then said, "Please don't be anxious or upset. I assure you I will take good care of you."

"I am neither anxious nor upset because there are people covering me with prayer and your hands are blessed."

His countenance seemed to change. "I am so glad to hear you say that because I pray for all my patients. God knows what He's doing," he said with a smile.

Forty eight hours later the surgery was done successfully. That was fifteen years ago. I learned my lessons; a few are patience, hope and faith. There have been many times when my faith has waned but after a while I would think back on the many things that God has brought me through and know God is always working on me from the inside out.

Stage Was Set

The play was about to start. The lights were switched on and off signaling the time to stop conversations. It was time to find my friend who had wandered off. I was annoyed that I had to wait for her. Janis arrived a bit late and out of breath.

"Where were you?" I asked, trying not to sound annoyed.

"I just had to speak to another friend I hadn't seen for a long time. Sorry," she said.

Janis was a good friend but she had the bad habit of always being late. We walked over many feet until we arrived at our seats. The theater was beautiful with colorful paintings of outdoor scenery. The curtains looked like heavy wine colored velvet. They were rope-tied gold ties that hung at the side of the curtains. All conversation stopped. There was a hush and the actors stepped on to the stage. I held on to my program tightly. I hadn't had a chance to read about the actors.

Janis had insisted I come and I didn't know anything about the play except it was a drama and the setting was a small town in the Midwest.

A man stepped out on stage. He was stunningly handsome. He wore blue jeans and a plaid shirt. For some reason he looked vaguely familiar. I couldn't hear his first lines because I heard the sound of loud ticking. Did Janis leave her I-phone on? The next person who stepped out on the stage was me! I couldn't believe it. I couldn't get my lines out. All that came out was a moan. Then I heard a loud sound. It was that old ugly clock with the bells on it. I woke up, thank goodness, just in time to "get on the other side of my coffee," as Ed Harris used to say, and get to writing class. I am glad that dream ended. I wouldn't want to go anywhere not knowing my lines, and certainly not in my nightgown.

The Jacket

S hopping isn't one of my favorite things to do but I had been invited to go on a bus trip with 24 ladies to go to seven resale shops. When they said resale that caught my attention. I am a bit frugal.

The first stop was a shop called Butterfly. We had coffee and were given a 15% discount. It was a beautiful sunny day.

"Aren't you going to buy anything, Phyllis?" my friend Delores asked.

"Maybe on the next stop."

We went to another shop. I didn't find anything there, either. It was time for our box lunch. I enjoyed lunch and the noise of ladies looking for a bargain.

Soon the bus was loaded with packages, even below the bus. I guess I'm not a veteran shopper like some.

Finally, we got to the last stop. I was exhausted from getting on and off of the bus. I asked myself was this a good idea? We were leaving the last place and outside on a rack there it was, in sartorial splendor, a black vision of loveliness, a plain jacket with a collar that stood up in a queenly way around the neck. Then I looked around and saw someone else trying on the same jacket. She looked nice in the jacket. She had wrinkled hands and crow's feet around her eyes. She looked pleasant and tired, too, but she was much older than me. I smiled at her and then I realized I was looking at my reflection in the store window. I did buy the jacket but I still don't like shopping. I might see my reflection again.

Resolution To Scratch

There is an itch that needs scratching. The itch of wanting to put things in order. My desk is out of order. My closet is out of order. My <u>emotions</u> are out of order. I spend lots of time thinking about how I can bring about order out of chaos. I suppose I must do it one step at a time. Even that requires an orderly and lucid mind; and I simply lack the energy. I must make myself devise a plan of action. Now what shall I do first? I will turn off the television and avoid reading negative news. Try as much as possible to avoid negative and boisterous people, they are a vexation to the soul. Clean everything off the tops of my desk and coffee table. Place it all in a box and resolve to only handle a piece of paper once. Go to the closet; place everything I haven't worn in three years in a bag. Take or send it to Goodwill. Get rid of books by taking them to the Library if I don't intend to read them again. Put high-heeled shoes in a box to be given away. Admit that I am a shoe-a-holic and get rid of the shoes. I know I will have withdrawal pains. Get more rest and make another admission; that is, that I am on emotional and physical overload. The most important of all, spend more time in meditation and prayer. I feel that I have filled in the dash of my life quite sufficiently. After I am gone, there will be many who will remember I was here. Can anyone ask for more? I absolutely resolve to take care of my itch. I have heard the saying, "scratch where it itches except in your britches." If it itches there, I will scratch there, too! This itch has gone on far too long. It's past time for action. Let the scratching begin!

Oops! I forgot about the messy bathroom.

May I Have This Dance?

I sat shyly, not knowing what to do. The party was pleasant. Everyone seemed to be having a good time. I was being ignored, as usual. My head was down. I tried to crawl within myself so nobody would see me.

I was dressed in a lovely pink ruffled dress with patent leather shoes. Why didn't anyone notice me? It's true, I really don't dance well.

Then I saw two big shiny shoes in front of me. I raised my head and there he was, tall and handsome. His smile could melt the heart of any girl, but he wanted to dance with me. I rose slowly to my feet and he said in a soft voice, "May I have this dance?"

"Oh yes," I said. I slipped off my patent leather shoes and stood on his feet just like we did at home.

We danced all over the room, swirling and dipping. He was the handsomest man in the room. I think about that night so often and I long to dance with my father just one more time. Sometimes when the house is quiet I can see us so plainly. He in his dark suit and tie and me in my pink ruffled dress and patent leather shoes!

"Dad, may I have just one more dance please?"

EVERY GOODBYE
AIN'T GONE

She Is More Than They Think

In Memory of my Mother,
Prudence Knox Adair, 1909-2003

Sunday afternoon has become my regular visit to see mother. She insists on cooking dinner for me every Sunday. It's her way of thanking me for the things I do for her. Of course, no thanks is necessary but it makes her feel needed; and so I let her.

I talk to her everyday to make sure she is all right. I used to call her a few times a week because she seemed self-willed and independent. A friend of hers, Gladys, called me a few years ago and told me that mother had called her crying, saying she was lonely. I was ashamed that I hadn't spent more time with her. Gladys told me how much mother loves me and how proud she is of me. She said mother was especially proud when I went to the president of the company that I worked for and told him I was offended by a picture in the cafeteria. The picture was of African-American people in a night club, appearing to be drunk, lying on tables and hanging off a balcony. Gladys said Prudence was afraid that I would lose my job. However, she was ecstatic when I wrote a scathing article to the Indianapolis Star about negative images of African-American people in art and in the media. I told Gladys I was surprised, not only had mother never told me she loved me (though I know she does), I didn't think she took any interest in the articles I wrote. When I read them to her, she would usually say, "That's nice, where did you learn those big words?" I didn't think, with her poor hearing, that she heard what I read. "She hears far more than you think," Gladys said. I think you're right! Thanks for calling and being such a good friend to mother. I will never neglect her again.

Mother is 88 years old and her age is beginning to show. Every time I see her, there are more signs of aging. When she was 85, her face was amazingly unwrinkled. After a bout with a kidney infection and pneumonia, wrinkles started to show around her chin. The skin sags on her neck because she lost thirty pounds. Her false teeth don't fit well and the clicking drives me crazy. "I can't hear it, so it doesn't matter; besides, another pair would be too expensive," she said. Her skin always appears dry. Her eyes look swollen. She has had cataract surgery on one eye. She said she might have the other one done when she's 95. Mother used to be tall, about 5'8". Now, her shoulders are rounded and she is a few inches shorter. Her right ankle turns down a bit and her walk is a shuffle. She uses a four-prong cane, which she calls "little boy." Her hair is black with a bit of gray that frames her face. Her voice is soft; she has quiet dignity.

Mother told me a few years ago that she didn't like to go to some restaurants because too many old people were there. "X Restaurant is especially depressing because there are more old people there than in a nursing home," she said with a grin. "How do you know when you are old?" I asked. With a twinkle in her eyes she said, "When you walk with a shuffle, complain a lot, you are extremely nosy, you can't remember what happened fifty minutes ago, but you can remember everything that happened fifty years ago." By her own description, she has become old. I am often amazed at her memory, delighted with her wit and humor, and devastated by what appears to be signs of dementia. Mother remembers to take her medication and all of her doctor appointments. She knows that when I take her to the doctor, I will also take her to lunch. So, she can be quite creative with her illnesses. Her ailments range from muscle aches to a pain in her big toe.

When I do the grocery shopping, she makes certain to only ask for enough groceries to last for one week. This is to assure that I will take her to the grocery the following week. I never let her know that I know what she is up to.

Lately, she wants to hear a full account of what I've done with my day. If my day isn't full of enough activity (writing doesn't count), there is a hint of disappointment in her voice as if I have wasted my day. When I ask her what she did with her day, she answers with an emphatic nothing! I think she has begun to live vicariously through me. She resents that she can no longer do all the things she used to do like reading books and the newspaper from cover to cover, traveling and working in her garden. I resent it, too.

Mother lives in a well-appointed apartment for senior citizens, which she keeps spotlessly clean. The residents are friendly and there are lots of planned activities; but mother doesn't interact much because she doesn't hear well. She does enjoy the Price is Right, Wheel of Fortune, Sixty Minutes, and religious programs on television. She regards the television remote control as a nuisance; knobs are better, she thinks. A few weeks ago, she started telling me about the lady in the apartment next to hers. She said the lady would talk to her through the wall and knew when she got in and out of bed. She said sometimes the lady will say, "Get up, Prudence. Get, up! Get up! It's time to take your shower!" She tells me every day what the lady next door is saying. One of the reasons I picked this senior facility for her is that it is practically fireproof. The walls between apartments are almost a foot thick. There is no possible way she can hear someone talking from another apartment. It would be difficult for a person with perfect hearing. I have tried to explain this to her, but to no avail. Is this an attempt to get more attention, or does she really believe the lady next door is harassing her? I asked her if she wanted me to talk to the lady next door. "No," she said. "I don't want you to upset her."

I suggested that she talk to the apartment manager, and she said the apartment manager laughed and said she must be imagining it and was probably having a reaction to her medication. The manager might have been right, but mother was very upset that the manager didn't believe her. Friends have told me this is just the beginning of a downward mental slide. I pray it is not so.

As if that were not enough to upset me, Mother told me that sometimes at church young people practically knock her down because she walks so slowly. They run past and shout, sorry, as they go, but never stop. I guess they don't know, she has been a member of that church more than 70 years and that she taught their parents and grandparents in Sunday school for 55 years. When she joined a Baptist church, there were 25 members; now, there are more than 6,000. Of course, they can't know.

The manager of the apartment building, the young people at church and others see mother as a frail old lady who can't hear well, or walk fast and who sometimes appears to be delusional. She is not who they think. I see her as a person who always gave, never expecting anything in return. One who can inspire without speaking simply by being. I see a little girl who left a prejudiced city 78 years ago, one step ahead of the Ku Klux Klan, to come to another city steeped in racism; but survived strong, proud, dignified, and loving. One able to forgive almost anything. When did you become the child again, mother; and when did I become the adult? Oh God, if I only had a weapon to fight this demon called dementia. I would fight with all my strength. It happened so subtlety, I didn't recognize it. I will never forget who you were, mother, and whose you are. I see far beyond what others see. You are more than they think, so much more.

Cousin Lorraine

I have been asked to give a tribute to honor Lorraine. Perhaps I was asked because I am the eldest female cousin.

Whatever the reason, I am privileged to attempt to do so. I wish I could express each cousin's thoughts. I can only share my own. In Thessalonians 5:18, it reads in everything give thanks, this is the will of God in Christ Jesus for you. And so we, the cousins of Lorraine Knox, and the descendants of William and Sallie Knox, give thanks for the treasured life of our beloved Lorraine.

A few weeks ago, I was placing pictures in an album. Among them were pictures of my mother and Lorraine on the occasion of mother's birthday. Mother and Lorraine were laughing so hard that it brought tears to their eyes and mine. It was as though they shared some juicy little secret only they knew about. What was it? I wondered. That was a wonderful day for all of us!

There are so many beautiful memories about Lorraine. She often said, "There is nothing we can't do. After all, we are Knox girls!" I believed her. She is so special. There is not one single word that can describe her. She IS sweet, dependable, attentive, loyal, intelligent, articulate, has a quick wit, a ready response, usually a funny one. One day we were talking. I don't remember what the conversation was about. I said, "Lorraine, don't you think you are a little bossy?"

She laughed and said, "Yes, and what is your point?" I laughed and said, "I guess I don't have one."

She IS a loving daughter, sister, aunt, sister-in-law, friend and cousin. Did you notice I said IS? Lorraine will never be WAS for me. I will never ever say goodbye. Our grandmother Knox used to say, "Every goodbye ain't gone." She has just slipped away, like she did at many family reunions. She will never be out of our hearts. As long as we hold her there, she will never be forgotten nor will any of our family.

I will not even say sleep well. I don't believe you are asleep, Lorraine, but greeting all those who have gone before and giving orders to those that will listen.

Lorraine, it fills my heart with so much joy knowing that you are safely in God's hands and in no more pain. Our last words in the hospital were:

"Lorraine, this is Phyllis."

It was more like a question with that soft sweet, yet strong voice you said, "Hello, Phyllis."

I said, "I love you." She knew that I will always say I love you.

"Give my love to everyone and tell them I said I love them, too."

In Revelations 3:8, it says, "See, I have set before you an open door." You, my Darling Lorraine, with all the elegance of a queen, just walked right through it!

Every Goodbye Ain't Gone

My Dearest friend and brother Yaji,

Did I spell your name correctly? You would feign insult if I didn't, but I have never written to you before.

Why did you have to go and change your name anyway? I thought John was just fine; that was the name you had when I met you more than ten years ago, or would you prefer that I call you Dr. McCurtis? You loved to make everything so complicated. Well, there I go with our usual little argument.

Why did you have to go anyway? I didn't even know. I knew you would get around to calling when you got good and ready. Of course, you would say, "YOUR ARMS AREN'T BROKEN YOU COULD HAVE CALLED ME." I hate to admit it, but you are right. I could get on with my life if I didn't hear your voice admonishing me for one thing or another.

We used to celebrate our birthdays together. Remember? You often gave me a book I didn't understand. When I told you that I didn't understand it, you gave me an expression that said, "Read it till you do," so I did. Being around you was always a fun and intellectual experience. Thanks for homeschooling me. You always told me, you were elitist and you were, but I would never tell you. I told you, you just kept getting doctorates because you were too lazy to get a real job. You loved it. Oh, how I miss our bantering and games of one-upmanship. I saw a mutual friend the other day and she asked, "Have you heard about Yaji?"

"Did the rascal leave town without telling me?"

"I thought he passed away," she said. I was stunned! How could my friend and brother pass away? I never told you I loved you as much as my own brother.

You were such a strong believer in always exercising and eating the right things. I will miss the invitations to your home for some exotic dish you so proudly prepared, Yaji. Most of all, I will just miss you. I must repeat the old adage my grandmother used to say because the grammar would be so offensive to you. Grandmother would say: Every goodbye ain't gone. I must say goodbye to you for a while my friend; but every goodbye ain't truly gone. You will always live in my heart. If that's all right with you.

With a sister's love,
Phyllis

Disty Girl

Dear Disty Girl,

Oh how I will miss our talks. You were never too tired or in too much pain to have a laugh, or two, or three, or four. Never in too much pain to give an encouraging word. I needed them often. We shared our joys and our sorrows, mostly joys.

You said whenever you were ill that Tom and I were there when you opened your eyes. We will always be there and you will always be right here in our hearts. How can we say good-bye? I can't! We will see you on every bright day. Remembering your special "laff" will warm us on cold days. There will never be a day that we won't remember you.

You were a wonderful, loving wife. A mother who was loved and honored by her children. A doting grandmother. A great-grandmother who thought her grandson was the most beautiful child in the world. I certainly would never contradict you; even though, I thought mine were the most beautiful. A friend to so many! We will miss you.

Above all, you are a child of God. And now, you are in God's loving arms, and in the company of all those who have gone on before. We are comforted knowing that one day, we shall behold "Him" face to face and one day we shall behold you face to face. That will be a glorious day!

Disty Girl, I will see you later.

Forgiven

They stood in the doorway of their home; a home that was once filled with so much joy and laughter.

"I guess this is the end," she said

"It doesn't have to be," he answered. Tears fell from their eyes. Their clothes were wet with tears.

"Can you ever forgive me?" he whispered.

"I want to, but things will never be the same. You lied and betrayed me so many times and I loved you so much! I guess I still do."

He took off his wedding band and placed it in her hand.

"I will always love you," he said choking back the tears. He walked out of the door. She leaned against the other side of the door shaking, and clutching the ring in her hand wanting to call him back, but she knew things between them would never change.

I can never forgive him, she thought. Years passed and their love for each never diminished. His home became a monument to her. He wanted to be forgiven.

Her monument to him was in her heart. She moved on with her life having forgiven him years ago. Perhaps, he never knew.

He Is Beautiful

In Memory of Ed Harris

I can see him in my mind so clearly. He was elegant. He was lovely. He looked as if he had climbed from a picture and stood before the congregation. His likeness should be framed and placed in a gallery of distinguished and worthy men.

We waited with bated breath for him to speak. Would his voice be low and commanding, or soft, not fitting my thoughts or his stature? Finally, he spoke. It was easy to detect that he was a southern gentleman and he was fiercely proud of it.

Who is this man? What is his story? I could tell by his look and the cadence of his voice that he was someone extraordinary. What is his name? Will imagining be better than finding out? I am determined to find out! Sometimes not knowing is better than knowing. Whether I find out everything or not, he will still be beautiful to me.

No amount of compensation seems adequate for the sacrifice [Ed] Harris endured for our nation during the civil rights movement, at great risk to his life, his family and livelihood. He is a man of uncommon peace, who yearns to share his life's mission of promoting respect among fellow men and racial reconciliation...He worked behind the scenes with the church to pull off the Selma to Montgomery March, which was led by Martin Luther King Jr....Harris states, "It is a process of starting again after failure. We can not always live up to our best selves

*but we can start over. We can change." The words of a
hero.*

James Patterson
A true civil rights hero who resisted the 'Southern Way'.
The Indianapolis Star

Ed Harris

I t's been more than 15 years since I met Ed.
Gone from this place, but never from my mind.
It was a meeting that changed my life in so many ways.
Ed befriended, mentored, challenged,
awed, surprised me with his enormous
lexicon of words. His ability to
write and tell a story in such
an excellent way. His deep humanity,
forthrightness, compassion, unselfishness
and indomitable spirit will never be
erased from the pages of my mind.

How Can I Say Goodbye?

I t's a beautiful fall day. The leaves are turning from green to gold. I think of so many past fall days, but today is different. Today, I must say goodbye to a loved one. I don't know how.

How would he want me to spend my morning? I think he would be very pleased to know that I'm doing just what I'm doing – thinking of him. I think of all the family reunions. He prepared many of the meals. What a grand chef he was, and no one could out-hug or out-smile him.

He loved life! When he was told that he had cancer, he accepted the news, not without dread, but with a triumphant spirit. He decided on no chemo and lived for two more birthdays. On the 4th of July, he turned sixty. What a celebration.

Today I will attend, along with my family, a celebration of your life. I'm not sure how to say goodbye, but I think that we said goodbye the last time I saw you. You looked up at me from your wheelchair and said, "I love you." Oh, I had then and have now so much love for you. I whispered in your ear, "Surely goodness and mercy will follow 'you' all the days of your life." Then I said, "What is the rest?" and you said, "And I shall dwell in the house of the Lord forever." I tried to hug your skeletal body. You were so thin. I said, "Goodbye, my dear!"

Perhaps, that's how I will say it today; not sadly, but like you triumphantly! Goodbye my dear! I pray we will see each other again someday.

ESSAYS

Sole Search

That's sole as in soles of shoes.

I have always been searching for something, not the least of which is shoes. Every day, I get up with one of my first decisions being what I am going to wear and what shoes. Thus, the sole search begins. It wouldn't be so difficult if I were not a recovering shoe-a-holic. I always have been. If you know of a twelve-step program, please let me know. I am much improved, however. I believe it's a problem inherited from my mother, who also loved shoes.

Shoes can be a great source of personal and world history. I have read that shoes can not only be an object of desire, but a work of art, a force for change, or even a fetish. It has been said, a woman who collects shoes is a frustrated traveler, and she is searching for enlightenment. I am guilty on both counts.

Do you remember your first pair of black patent leather shoes with the grosgrain ribbon and straps around the ankle, or the black and white saddle oxfords, or penny loafers, or your first pair of high-heeled shoes? I sure do. I remember all of the times and places that I walked in those shoes. Did you have your children's shoes bronzed and now wonder if they were ever that small? I have shoes with heels so high I cannot possibly wear them, but I can't throw them away.

Yes, I have a passion for shoes!

When I was in a shoe store in Spain, the salesperson would only bring out the shoe for the right foot. I have a collection of miniature shoes.

In the case of these miniatures, there is no left shoe, they only sell the right shoe. The detail, style, and color of the miniature shoes are intriguing. I have a small collection. I collect all kinds of shoes, glass ones, ones made out of candles, and vintage ones.

Jan Ernst Matzelinger was born in 1852 in Surinam (Dutch Guinea, South America). His father was a Dutch engineer, married to a native black Surinamese woman. When he was 19, Jan Matzelinger left to seek his fortune and settled in Philadelphia two years later. He then went to Massachusetts searching for a better job. This was an almost impossible task as he spoke little English, but he quickly learned. He found a job as an apprentice in a shoe factory operating a sole sewing machine. In the early days of shoemaking, shoes were made by hand. The most difficult part of shoemaking was attaching the sole to the upper part of the shoe. It required great skill.

Because of his mechanical aptitude and fortitude, Matzelinger set out to invent a machine that would mass produce shoes. He secretly experimented on wooden and scrap iron models. He worked on the shoe machine for 10 years. In 1882, Matzelinger felt his machine would work. He applied for a patent and sent diagrams to Washington. The plans were so complicated that a patent officer was sent from Washington to see the machine. Matzelinger's machine could turn out 150-700 pairs of shoes a day, compared to the 50 pairs that were handmade. His shoe machine revolutionized the shoe industry for men and women in the United States and around the world. The demand for the machine was overwhelming.

Unfortunately, Matzelinger died in 1889 at the age of 37. He had worked long, hard hours without thought of his health. He also was a gifted artist and had numerous other inventions. He was rarely mentioned in history books. I am very grateful to Matzelinger for his outstanding contribution.

I know a few men who have a thing for shoes. I have a friend, Ed Harris, whose father owned a shoe store. He said his father called himself an "ole shoe dog." He loved the smell of the leather and the shape of the shoes. My friend was given many lessons on how to polish and care for shoes. His father definitely had a major thing for shoes.

Shoes, from the beginning of time, have always defined culture and history and made us aware of the times.

Shoes can definitely reflect your personality and an image you may want to portray. They make a statement about the wearer. The occasion dictates the type of shoes you wear. For instance, for a party, you may wear high-heeled, strappy sandals (that you know hurt); for the office, simple medium-heeled shoes; for walking, maybe tennis shoes for the beach, rubber flip flops; and for lounging at home, cuddled up in front of the fireplace with a good book, you many want pink fuzzy house shoes, warm and soft as a puppy. I am constantly searching for just the right shoes, not only for my collection, but ones that are comfortable and attractive. Perhaps, you are, too. There is a Buddhist saying, "When the shoe fits, the foot forgets the shoe." So…If you find the shoe that fits, may I suggest, by all means wear it!

What's In Your Cup?

I want to know! Why? You might ask. As I grow older, I have more questions than answers, and a few are: How do moths know where your best wool clothes are? Why is it if you are in the grocery line for 15 or less items, there is someone in front of you with 25 items? Why does my doctor look like she is 16 years old? And the question, "What's in 'your' cup?" have been added to the list.

Is tea what's in your cup? Are you among the millions all over the world who love a hot cup of tea? You could probably float a number of ocean liners in just a portion of the tea consumed around the world.

Tea was the main beverage served in coffeehouses, though coffee arrived in England many years before tea. The coffeehouses were exclusively for men. Teahouses were called "Penny Universities" because a pot of tea and a newspaper could be bought for a penny. They were the gentleman's private club. The English had Tea Gardens. Here ladies and gentlemen enjoyed tea outdoors. They had orchestras, arbors, concerts, fireworks, and gambling. Here ladies mixed publicly with men without criticism. The British mixed for the first time across lines of gender and station.

Tipping was first used in the Tea Gardens in England. A small wooden box would be placed on each table at the Tea Garden. On each box were the letters "TIPS," which stood for To Insure Prompt Service. If a guest wanted to insure prompt service and to make sure the tea arrived hot, a coin would be dropped into the box upon arrival. This custom has continued to this day.

When I visited Northern Georgia for the first time, I was fascinated by a leafy vine that appeared to be growing everywhere. The vines covered telephone poles, pine trees, barns, or whatever was in its path.

The vine is called Kudzu. Kudzu was used for ground cover and grows extremely well in the southern states. It has been said, "If you don't close your windows, it will come right in." I have never had Kudzu tea. I look forward to that.

I have recently discovered a tea called rooibos (roy boss), which comes from Kenya. When left in the sun, it turns from green to red. Rooibos is often referred to as a redbush and was unheard of for centuries.

It is naturally sweet and can be used for many purposes. Rooibos has become one of the most consumed teas in the world. If you haven't tried it yet, you will be pleased with the delicious red beverage.

There are myriad of uses for tea.

Tea can be used cosmetically. To cool off during the hot summer months, pour one or two cups of brewed tea into warm bath water. The tea is not only refreshing, but it can soften the skin. You can temporarily streak your hair with a tea rinse. Shampoo as you normally do, then rinse with plain water. Next, rinse with brewed black tea that has been cooled. Leave in for five minutes. Squeeze out as much liquid as possible. Let your hair dry naturally. Your hair should be darker and shinier. If this doesn't work, you didn't hear it from me.

There are volumes that have been and can be written about tea. When I was a child, my grandmother insisted that her grandchildren drink sassafras tea. She told us sassafras thinned the blood. I have yet to understand why our blood needed thinning and how it got thick during the winter, but this was one of the rites of spring. As soon as the forsythia arrived, out came the sassafras. It was a family ritual that we were happy to partake in. It certainly was better than castor oil, which also was given as a spring tonic. Maybe granny knew something we didn't. It has been recorded that sassafras was America's first tea. Every spring, I get the urge for sassafras tea. Spring is here! Maybe sassafras is in your cup.

I can think of no better way to slow down and enjoy life's special moments than over a cup of tea. Tea creates an ocean of calm. Every day is a good day for tea, so I invite you to pick a day, any day. Today would be good. Find a comfortable place, fill your cup with your favorite beverage, stir in kindness, and pour sweetness to taste. Take a big sip, lift your cup in celebration of yourself, and have a Beau-Tea-ful day!

Dreaming From A Chinaberry Tree

I have always had a love affair with trees. I love the acacia, elm, maple and the weeping willow tree most of all. I am not alone. Many poems, stories and books have been written about trees. One of my favorite poems I learned as a child is by Joyce Kilmer.

It was even turned into a song. I'm sure you know both. I recited and said this poem 'til friends and family pleaded with me to cease and desist. I answered by saying, "but she is such a good poet." I was trying to sound grown up.

A cousin said, "Joyce Kilmer is not a she. Joyce Kilmer is a man.

"You're not telling the truth. Joyce is a girl's name."

"We have an uncle named Shirley, and a cousin named after him, Shirley, Jr. So why do you think Joyce is just a girl's name?"

I stomped off to talk with mother about it.

I have always been a dreamer. As a child, I tried the patience of everyone with my incessant questions. Why this? Why that? Not much has changed.

When I wanted to daydream, after everyone had grown bone weary with my questions, I sat under my grandmother's weeping willow tree. I wondered how children in other countries lived and what "they" thought about. I remembered a story that I heard about the Israelites hanging their harps on a willow tree and refusing to sing. Why did they do that? I wondered.

My mother told me about pine trees in the woods of Georgia where she was born. My grandfather would cut them down and use them for Christmas trees. She talked about peach trees and persimmon trees, but she never mentioned a chinaberry tree; and I have never seen one.

A chinaberry tree, from what I have read, looks like a great place for dreaming! It has clusters of purplish flowers; however, the small fruit of the tree is highly poisonous. Bees and butterflies are not attracted to the chinaberry. Chinaberry trees grow tall and provide shade.

Now that I've told you about a chinaberry tree, I will tell you a bit about the life and times of a little eight-year-old who started her dreaming from a chinaberry tree.

The little girl climbed high in the chinaberry tree next to the gate of her home. She tried to see to the end of the horizon and beyond. She wondered where her life would take her and she was anxious to get there. She was born in Alabama. Before I tell you her name, I will tell you about her parents and her childhood.

The little girl who dreamed from the chinaberry tree grew up in an eight-room house, surrounded by five acres of land with fruit trees. Her father was a preacher and carpenter. Her mother became a teacher who encouraged her to set her goals high. She was the granddaughter of enslaved Georgians. Her mother's name was Lucy and her father's name was John. She was the second daughter and the fifth child of eight.

John asked Lucy to marry him. Her parents did not approve. In spite of their objections, Lucy married John.

When Lucy was pregnant with her fifth child, she unexpectedly went into labor while her husband was away.

A few days later, a neighbor and friend of Lucy's reminded her of the promise she had made to allow her to name the baby if it was a girl. She named the baby Zora.

When Zora was around nine, her mother passed away. The ending of her mother's life was the beginning of turmoil for feisty Zora. To Zora and her siblings' disgust and hurt, their father married shortly thereafter. The new wife was jealous, contentious and could not tolerate spirited, sassy Zora. They fought verbally and physically. Zora was sent to Jacksonville with her brother.

Jacksonville was different for Zora in so many ways. She could no longer go into a grocery store and receive candy just because she was a smart little girl. She couldn't hang around and listen to the adults talk, fight with boys, or dream from the chinaberry tree.

At her new school, the girls didn't appreciate her always talking and being in their way. Most of the teachers were pleased with her as Zora was a good student and always won the spelling bee contests.

Zora's father abandoned her. She was shifted from one relative to another. She longed for school. She found a worn book of Milton's work and she spent days devouring every word of Milton's epic poem book *Paradise Lost*. Zora had become a teenager and needed to work. She found a job working for an actress. During that time, she had the chance to travel and be exposed to the opera and classical music.

One of the men from a singing group loaned Zora books, which she read voraciously. Her new and wonderful world came to an end when her employer left to get married. Zora had to find another job. She worked and attended night school. One evening, she heard her instructor read Kubla Khan; she was mesmerized and vowed that she would get an education.

After graduation, she attended Howard University. She loved literary discussion and was selected to be a member of a literary group.

Earning her degree was difficult as coming up with money for tuition was nearly impossible. However, she had written short stories and a play. An editor of a magazine who was interested in talented black writers used some of her work.

Zora was a fascinating storyteller. She drew her stories from the colorful people from her hometown. Suddenly, Zora became a star and a sought out guest at the homes of prominent families.

She attended college and studied anthropology on a scholarship arranged for her by the founder of the college. She often frequented get-togethers with writers, artists and musicians.

Zora wrote many short stories, which were published and well accepted by some. She began to pursue her interest in anthropology with the help of a prominent anthropologist. Now she could apply a scientific approach to her interest in folklore. Zora returned to Florida to record the stories she had heard as a child. After six months of collecting information, she traveled back to New York. Her research was published.

The book was a success but an attempt at a musical failed. Zora returned to home to rest and write more stories.

Zora took a job as a drama teacher at a college in Ohio. The money she earned from her book soon ran out. She was awarded a fellowship to get a doctorate in anthropology.

She grew restless, didn't attend class. Zora received a another fellowship. After receipt of the fellowship, she went to the Caribbean to study. While there she met medicine men, went on wild boar hunts and witnessed and participated in voodoo rites.

Zora's next two books, one based on voodoo practices that she studied and the other, her version of the biblical Moses, both met with mixed reviews. Frustrated by trying to be all things to all people, she sought solace on a houseboat that she bought in Florida. She continued writing and produced another book.

Zora found some semblance of solitude on her houseboat but she was ill and needed money. She took jobs as a freelance writer for a newspaper, did substitute teaching and was a librarian. She always returned to her passion for writing. Although rejection letters piled up, she was resolute. After suffering a stroke, she passed away in 1960.

Zora Neale Hurston wrote seven books. Her published short stories are too numerous to list. She also produced musicals and was a successful anthropologist.

Zora Neale Hurston lamented that she wished she could write all of her books over again. I understand her feeling. I think that if she had rewritten her books, she might not have been as creative and honest. Had she written any other way during those times, her work would have been totally unacceptable by those with the wherewithal to produce it. She was a brilliant woman, trying to straddle two worlds and dealing with criticism from both.

My mother taught me to love and appreciate the arts; to carefully evaluate things I don't understand or agree with. I am enamored with the melodious sound of the white and black southern dialect and learned to read it and to speak it, and also to love Bach, Beethoven, and Negro spirituals. All of these things can stir my thoughts of fulfilled and unfulfilled dreams. I love dreamers!

Today Zora would have been shunned for her political incorrectness. By many accounts, at times she could be manipulative and always controversial. At other times, charming, gentle, generous and always extremely intelligent. She was quite an enigma. I stand in awe of her wit, animus, and audacity. She made many of her dreams from a chinaberry tree come true.

Though Zora Neale Hurston did not accomplish all that she wanted to do, a part of her lives on. It is a tradition in my family that you say the name of someone you admire so they won't be forgotten. I must admit, I really do love Zora Neale Hurston, the chinaberry dreamer.

Pockets

I am approaching a birthday.

I think of so many things in the recesses and pockets of my mind and heart. The number of calendar years that add up my life seem almost unbelievable to me. I have lived a long time. Longer than many of my friends. There are so many memories.

I can remember hearing about the bombing of Pearl Harbor and being too young to understand what that meant. I remember the sound of President Roosevelt's voice coming from our large RCA radio. I can remember all of the voices of American presidents thereafter.

I remember wars and jingles about wars and old songs about wars.

I remember untrue friends, loneliness, duplicity and fear of what the future would bring.

The future is now and I will try to button down the bad memories because they make me sad. The pockets that bring me joy I will unbutton wider!

I look forward to birthdays now. At one time I found it depressing that I was growing older. Now for me it is simply a number assigned to me for statistics.

Though my outer body shows signs of aging, my inner body soars like an eagle. My steps are like that of a deer. There are many who will disagree with that. That's just dreaming and believing for the best, even though the circumstances might indicate otherwise. *"(As it is written…) even God, who quickeneth the dead, and calleth those things which be not as though they were."* – Romans 4:17 – King James Version (KJV)

On my birthday, I celebrate by giving a gift to someone I don't know. It could be someone I see in a restaurant or someone at a shop. I tell them it is my birthday and I want to share it by giving them a gift.

It is fantastic to see that moment of surprise when I hand them the gift. For that moment they may see beyond the gray hair and wrinkles to a heart that tries to open the pockets of joy in others. Try it. It feels so good!

Editor's Note

This autobiographical presentation of short stories, vignettes, poetry, and keen insights into life's precious journey can evoke a range of emotions in the reader from exuberant joy to endearing sadness to contemplative reflection. The essays in the final section of this book are abbreviated. If you would like to read the full versions, they can be found in the Indiana Historical Society archives.

Beyond the Wind Chimes is Phyllis' second book, a gem never to be forgotten and in my view even more intriguing than her first, *Wind Chimes and Promises*, a portion of which was made into a play and shown on television. Both will be cherished by book readers for a long time to come. I hope that you enjoy the stories as much as I do. God changes not.

James Patterson, former Editorial Writer, The Indianapolis Star

Reflections

J oye M. Carter, MD

I can sit for hours over a cup of tea and talk to Phyllis about almost any topic. She is such a great storyteller and there is always a lesson to be learned.

Phyllis' new book is so much like her personality, full of mirth, a history lesson, nurturing words and a brief glimpse into a remarkable mind. The story of "Fifty-four" made me smile and remember what I was thinking at that age and what I could expect to come to mind as I move into my next phase of life.

I was sitting in a tea shop on a winter's day in midtown Indianapolis, with my mother in early 2007. The weather was brisk outside and we had just come from a doctor's appointment. The atmosphere was gray and I was exhausted from a long day of work as well as braving the parking and crowds in the medical center. Suddenly, the door to the restaurant swung open and a lovely woman was standing in the doorway asking for the manager. All eyes were upon this woman as she asked the manager for the residual number of her books.

This silver-haired beauty had an air of knowledge and wisdom that when combined made the statement of "Do Not Mess With Me," and I immediately wanted to get to know her. I struck up a conversation about writing and that began a journey of friendship and love that remains unstoppable and has become woven into the fabric of my daily sense of wellbeing.

Mother Phyllis, as I affectionately call her now, is a woman of many talents. As I have referenced before, she has much wisdom. She has a sense of humor and depth of spirituality that I am able to borrow when I feel like I cannot attempt to go another step. I know that when I am bothered by an emotional event, I can call her for a word of prayer and a heart-warming hug.

A few days after we met, we exchanged books and I learned the value of hard work and family structure from reading her first book, *Wind Chimes and Promises.* We shared in common the painful bond of losing a mother to the theft of Alzheimer's disease. When others failed me, I knew I could run into the arms of Mother Phyllis, who always had a kind word and would make time to listen to my concerns.

This woman is so energetic and full of life, I have to keep up with her. Her sense of style and natural beauty makes me look forward to aging in her same graceful pattern.

Printed in the United States
By Bookmasters